"Infidelity doesn't have to be the end of the road, even though it often feels that way. Couples can, and do, often find their way to an ultimately deeper, more intimate bond, and I can think of no better guide to lead the journey than Tammy Nelson."

> —Ian Kerner, PhD, sex therapist and *New York Times* bestselling author of *She Comes First*

"*The New Monogamy* takes an honest look at infidelity and illustrates a clear path toward healing after an affair."

> —John Gray, PhD, author of *Men Are from Mars, Women Are from Venus*

"*The New Monogamy* sets Tammy Nelson apart from many other therapists. She doesn't believe affairs simply involve a pathetic victim and an arrogant perpetrator—and that's why she can actually help couples navigate this difficult challenge."

> —Marty Klein, PhD, author of *Sexual Intelligence*

"Provocative and juicy, far-reaching and intelligent."

> —Janis Abrahms Spring, author of *After the Affair* and *How Can I Forgive You?*

"This book is a game changer for couples dealing with the aftermath of an affair. It is unique in offering hope that this experience can be used to build a new and *better* relationship. But it offers far more than just hope; it provides detailed guidelines for how to make it happen. Tammy Nelson is a visionary in going beyond the immediate need to develop a new monogamy agreement to include the all-important process of revisiting and revising this agreement over time."

—Peggy Vaughan, author of *The Monogamy Myth*
and host of dearpeggy.com

"Tammy Nelson is a master therapist who can help you find hope and opportunity in the multiple crises caused by an affair. *The New Monogamy* offers safe, effective steps through the confusion, betrayal, and hurt—with guidelines for how you can create more honest, erotic, and soul-satisfying relationships."

—Gina Ogden, PhD, LMFT, author of *The Return of Desire* and *The Heart & Soul of Sex*

"At a time when life can feel so murky and chaotic, along comes Tammy Nelson with this guidebook…. *The New Monogamy* is as crisp and clear as it is hopeful and realistic. A book to open again and again."

—Esther Perel, author of *Mating in Captivity*

The NEW MONOGAMY

REDEFINING YOUR

RELATIONSHIP

AFTER INFIDELITY

TAMMY NELSON, PhD

New Harbinger Publications, Inc.

Publisher's Note

This publication is designed to provide accurate and authoritative information in regard to the subject matter covered. It is sold with the understanding that the publisher is not engaged in rendering psychological, financial, legal, or other professional services. If expert assistance or counseling is needed, the services of a competent professional should be sought.

Distributed in Canada by Raincoast Books

Copyright © 2012 by Tammy Nelson
New Harbinger Publications, Inc.
5674 Shattuck Avenue
Oakland, CA 94609
www.newharbinger.com

Cover design by Amy Shoup
Acquired by Tesilya Hanauer
Text design by Tracy Marie Carlson
Edited by Nelda Street

Library of Congress Cataloging in Publication Data

Nelson, Tammy.
  The new monogamy : redefining your relationship after infidelity / Tammy Nelson, PhD.
    pages cm
  Includes bibliographical references.
    ISBN 978-1-60882-315-4 (pbk. : alk. paper) -- ISBN 978-1-60882-316-1 (pdf e-book) (print) -- ISBN 978-1-60882-317-8 (epub) (print) 1. Adultery--Psychological aspects. 2. Marital conflict. 3. Intimacy (Psychology) 4. Trust. I. Title.
  HQ806.N45 2013
  306.73'6--dc23

                              2012034635

Printed in the United States of America

14   13   12

10   9   8   7   6   5   4   3   2   1

First printing

This book is dedicated to all of my family, who I hope will always know that I love them above all else.

To Tyler and Emma, who are in my heart always, thank you for understanding that, although my work is my mission, you are my whole life.

To Nicole and Lauren, thank you for opening your hearts to me and letting me love you.

To my monogamous husband, Bruce, I have loved you for a thousand years and will love you for a thousand more.

Contents

Acknowledgments

Thanks so much to Melissa Kirk for her ceaseless and tireless editing, and her deep understanding of the subject matter. Thanks to Tesilya Hanauer for believing in me after reading my original article, "The New Monogamy," in *Psychotherapy Networker* magazine (2010), and thanks to Rich Simon for publishing that article; Rich is the kingmaker. Thanks to Nelda Street, Jess Beebe, Nicola Skidmore, Melissa Valentine, Adia Colar, Amy Shoup, Will DeRooy, and everyone at New Harbinger Publications for making this book happen.

Thanks to my assistant, Inara DeLuna (a.k.a. Rebecca Emberger), for being my assistant extraordinaire. Thanks to Harville Hendrix and Helen Hunt for their work in spreading Imago Relationship Therapy and for all that it has given me and my relationships. Thanks to Gina Ogden, Esther Perel, Janis Abrahms Spring, and Peggy Vaughan for everything they have taught me. Thanks to all of my clients, who have shown me what it means to do the work.

Thank you to Doug and Andy (show 'em how it's done!) Thanks to my sister, Melanie Barnum, for her support and love, without which I wouldn't always be so inspired.

Introduction

We live in a culture where almost 50 percent of married people get divorced and second marriages end at a rate of over 70 percent. Many of these marriages, perhaps as many as one-third, end because of infidelity. Are affairs a natural result of long-term relationships? Does this mean that as a society, we are not committed to monogamy?

Although studies vary, research shows that almost 60 percent of men and over 45 percent of women will cheat at some point in their marriages (Atwood and Schwartz 2002). Affairs affect 1 out of every 2.7 couples, which is almost one-third of all of us (Spring 1996).

Much of the literature on affair recovery assumes that infidelity is a symptom of some fundamental problem in a marriage or committed relationship, ignoring the more important dilemma of whether monogamy is even possible for the average person. Are over half of us just chronically bad at choosing our mates?

Yet cheating doesn't seem to make us happy either. We don't spend very much time in affairs: 10 percent of extramarital dalliances last only one day; another 10 percent last less than a month; and the rest last, at most, a year or two. Few extramarital affairs last longer than four years (ibid.). So, if affairs last an average of three years at most, do they work?

It turns out that only a handful of cheaters end up with their lovers. Only 3 percent of men marry the women they have affairs with, and the divorce rate is high (about 75 percent) among those who do marry their affair partners (Halper 1988). It seems that having an affair does not, in fact, create lasting happiness.

That makes sense, because unhappiness is not always the cause of affairs. In fact, studies show that up to 56 percent of men and 34 percent of women who were cheating described themselves at the time as being in happy marriages. They also said that they loved their primary partners and had good sex with them (Ben-Zeev 2008).

Staying committed to one partner for many years isn't easy. Couples in long-term, committed relationships have to learn many difficult relationship skills, including frustration tolerance, self-control, patience, conscious empathy, and, perhaps the most important skill of all, kindness.

The affair that has affected your relationship and brought you to pick up this book has undoubtedly been a supremely painful episode, one from which you may not be recovered and may never even recover fully. You will never be the same person as you were before the affair, and your relationship will never be the same relationship as it was. Although this may be painful to hear, the good news is that you now have the opportunity to create a better, stronger, more vibrant relationship with your current partner, if you are both committed to working through the issues that the affair has brought up.

Why This Book?

What if you could have a whole new marriage or committed relationship with your current partner? Is it possible that, despite the incredible pain of the infidelity that has affected your relationship, the affair was a wake-up call? Can you imagine creating a new relationship that works better for both of you? This book will show you how to make this a reality, by walking you through the steps to creating a *new monogamy*: a new relationship in which the needs and desires of both of you are explicitly stated and totally validated.

In the new monogamy, together, you get to create a relationship that works for both of you, regardless of cultural norms or expectations, as long as the terms are explicitly stated and agreed on by both of you. This book introduces vital tools for communicating with one another about your new monogamy, and gives you both the opportunity to really talk, honestly and perhaps more openly than you ever have, about your needs in this new style of relationship.

Is This Book for You?

This book is for anyone who has experienced betrayal and wondered how to make the current relationship better instead of ending it altogether. These tools work whether you are a heterosexual couple or a gay or lesbian couple, and whether you are officially married or in a committed partnership.

You can also benefit from this book if you are trying to decide whether or not to move on after an affair. If you haven't yet made up your mind whether to stay with your partner, this book can help you decide. And it can help you move on with your life in the aftermath. It may also tell you what you will need to know for your next relationship. Creating a new monogamy is an important goal for anyone who wants to start over.

Most of the exercises in this book are designed for you to do with your partner. I will introduce dialogues, checklists, and questionnaires that ask both of you to discuss issues in your relationship, how the affair affected you both, and what you each want from your ideal marriage. While it's possible for you to work through this book without your partner, you will both get more out of it if you work through it together. If your partner doesn't want to work with you, you may also rely on the help of a therapist, practicing the communication skills and answering the questions for yourself. However, if your partner is not willing, at any time, to work together with you on a new monogamy agreement, it may be prudent to consider whether you might be better off leaving the relationship. This will be discussed in the book, and it would be a good issue to bring to your therapist.

As you work through the book, both you and your partner should keep a handwritten or computer journal, where you record your responses, as well as your thoughts, emotions, and experiences as you go through the dialogues. This work will likely bring up some emotional issues, and keeping a record of these experiences will benefit both you and your relationship.

You are undertaking an important journey, one that has the potential to strengthen your relationship and bring you and your partner closer together than ever before. It will also help you explore your own needs and desires and get clear about what you really want in an intimate relationship. This will benefit you regardless of whether you ultimately stay with your partner.

About the Author

I have worked for many years with couples struggling with the seemingly impossible task of recovering from infidelity. While it may seem that affairs are one place where couples encounter a total impasse in therapy, I slowly discovered over weeks and months that the real tragedy for many of them was that they didn't really want to break up. They just felt they had no other choice.

It made sense that the only decision open to them was *when* to leave, not *if* they should leave. They had no other information or support that helped them to stay. Seeing how common affairs were in marriages and committed partnerships, I started to wonder not only why infidelity happened but also how I could help couples recover instead of break up.

In our society, an affair is usually either a make-or-break mistake or a "can opener": a way to get out of a marriage. Affairs are not usually seen as a way to "wake up" a marriage or turn it around. I started getting curious about this and began to challenge my own inclination to feel hopeless about relationships involving infidelity. I tried not to look at affairs as the result of a bad partner doing something to a good partner, or a pathology that had to be fixed or medicated away. I began to open my mind to the deep hurt and wounding that lay just under the surface of both partners, not just after the affair but also before it even began.

I began challenging my clients to imagine and envision what it would be like to stay together after an affair. I wondered what it would take. I looked at the work I had done with couples up to that point, and knew that the couples that had stayed together the longest and reported being the happiest were those who had passionate sex and were erotically and intimately connected. I knew this would be important in long-term relationships after infidelity as well.

Yet sex after an affair is difficult at best. Erotic recovery, something I will discuss in chapter 6, is complicated and painful. I tried to understand that trust is not always about one partner being apologetic, but about both partners learning to trust themselves again. I watched as, together, my clients and I created a new vision of a new type of relationship: a brand-new monogamy. And it began to work. Couples made it work. I saw that not only was it possible to survive an affair but also these couples did better than ever. They were happier, calmer, and more connected than before the affair.

I wrote this book to challenge the common view that an affair has to mean the end of a relationship. Monogamy as we know it is changing in our world and in our culture. Our ability to remain monogamous is becoming more difficult in an age when cheating is easier than ever. Marriage as we know it will be totally different by the end of this century. The couples that manage to stay together and make it work will be the ones who decide to create fluidity and flexibility in their partnerships, and find ways to make monogamy work for them.

What This Book Covers

This book is designed to take you through the steps of creating a new monogamy agreement that will help you make your relationship expectations more explicit. In this way, any misunderstandings, resentments, unspoken issues, and assumptions that may have been at the root of the affair won't have a chance to negatively affect your new relationship, and your future together will be more honest and open as a result.

Chapter 1 explains the new monogamy, and how your and your partner's explicit and implicit expectations about your relationship may be contributing to its breakdown. Chapter 2 shows you how to explore the affair with your partner to understand why it happened, what both of your experiences were of the infidelity, and how those experiences affected both of you.

By learning from the affair, you and your partner will have a head start on creating a new relationship in which the needs and desires of both of you are taken into consideration. Chapter 3 discusses the importance of trust and empathy in working with your internal experience and with your partner's experience of the affair, in order to build a new foundation of acceptance and openness in your relationship. Although you don't have to forgive your partner, you do have to cultivate empathy and self-trust after this traumatic event, if you are to develop a positive, stable relationship in the future.

Chapter 4 leads you through some explorations of what you want to have in your relationship going forward, including ideas and desires you may or may not have shared with your partner before. Chapter 5 helps you and your partner develop your new monogamy agreement through open and honest dialogues about what you both really want to experience in your relationship. Although these conversations can be difficult and emotional, you will find that if you approach them with curiosity and compassion, they may bring you and your partner closer together, perhaps closer than you've ever been. Chapter 6 presents the steps to erotic recovery, a crucial part of healing from an affair and recommitting to nurturing sexual connection with your partner. Chapter 7 offers even more tips for reconnecting erotically, and chapter 8 concludes the book, offering hope for your new monogamy and insight into how marriage is changing in our culture.

In short, this book will help you create a living, evolving relationship with your current partner, not only despite the affair, but also perhaps because of it. The affair can help you both learn more about yourselves and each other.

Most likely you are still upset, hurt, and resentful that your partner cheated, and you may find yourself overwhelmed, emotional, or even angry when you read that you need to develop compassion and empathy for your partner's experience in order to develop a strong relationship in the future. These responses are normal and understandable. You never have to be happy about the affair, but I will ask you to keep an open mind and a sense of curiosity as you read through this book. Nobody wants to be cheated on, but as I've heard many, many times in my work with clients affected by infidelity, the affair can be the wake-up call that makes your relationship stronger, more open, and more alive with passion and intimate connection than ever before. I wish the same for you and your partner as you move forward into *your* new monogamy!

CHAPTER 1

Infidelity and the New Monogamy

So your partner had an affair and now you are wondering what to do about it. Does infidelity always have to mean the end of the relationship? Perhaps you are considering other options before starting divorce proceedings; maybe you are even thinking about staying with your spouse. You may instinctively know already that infidelity is much more complicated than our culture sometimes admits, and that there may be more choices in the aftermath of an affair than just divorcing or permanently ending your relationship. This book can help you decide whether staying is the right thing to do.

Affairs can be painful and shocking, and can often cause untold damage. However, this book may show you that for some couples, an affair may also be a path to strength and to a renewed and even stronger relationship. If both of you can approach healing and reconciliation with deep honesty, even in the face of some serious pain, you may be able to realize this vision.

If either of you is on the fence about whether or not to stay together, this book can show you what to do, step by step, in exploring the option of giving your relationship another chance.

The Three Components of an Affair

By its nature, infidelity has three elements, any of which can be devastating, depending on how it affects you and your marriage. Some people feel betrayed in one area more than in others. The three parts of an affair are:

- The outside emotional relationship

- The dishonesty

- The sexual relationship

An affair can include only one of these aspects and still be devastating, such as when your partner has a nonsexual emotional affair. Or it can include two areas, as in a hidden sexual affair that has no emotional relationship, perhaps with a sex worker. An online relationship may include some dishonesty while never developing into anything sexual or emotional, but by virtue of its hidden nature or the lies your partner tells to cover it up, you can feel very betrayed by your partner's cyber connection. Or an affair can include all three parts.

Affairs most commonly include each of these elements on some level. All of these areas may be problematic for you, or only one area may be really upsetting. Of course, reactions can vary for each situation.

The Outside Emotional Relationship

An outside emotional relationship can be any type of strong emotional connection that is formed with someone outside of your primary partnership and goes deeper than simply a normal friendship. This emotional relationship becomes a betrayal when it crosses a line of intimacy that makes the other person equally or more important to your partner than you are. You may feel left out and hurt by your partner's affection for this other person, and this can feel like a threat to your relationship.

Finding out about an outside relationship that your partner is having that doesn't include you may affect your future ability to trust your partner to ever have friends outside of your marriage. If your partner shared deep, personal secrets with that outside person, you may feel that your own relationship is now less emotionally intimate and less of a priority for your partner.

The Dishonesty

The dishonesty is the lying, denying, or hiding of an affair that makes it difficult to later trust your partner in deep and meaningful ways. If you discovered your partner's affair by accident and had to confront her, you may feel betrayed that she never came to you directly with the truth. If, when confronted, your partner denied the evidence, you may wonder how you can continue being with someone who lied to your face. If your partner insisted that you were imagining it when you confronted her about the affair, you may feel hopeless about her capacity to ever be honest with you. If your partner admits to the affair or even confesses, you may be shocked that she could have so easily hidden parts of herself all this time and that she could lie to you by omission.

The Sexual Relationship

The sexual-relationship aspect of the affair can be the deepest injury for some. You may feel that the sexual betrayal creates the deepest wound to your sexual self-esteem. Knowing that your partner crossed the line of physical intimacy with someone else may hurt you deeply. Because this is a difficult betrayal to get past, I will spend a lot of time in this book talking about the erotic injury to your relationship and how to heal from it.

Some people have the capacity to compartmentalize their erotic experience and keep it separate from their feelings for their partners. When your partner says, "The sex meant nothing," he may be telling you the truth. Casual sex, cybersex, or erotic encounters with paid sex workers are sometimes put into this category. However, this doesn't make it any less painful for the partner who discovers the affair.

Your reactions and feelings when you find out about your partner's affair are valid. Allow yourself to experience whatever emotions you have in reaction to each of these three types of betrayal. All of your feelings are normal; it's what you do with your feelings that can either be helpful or harmful.

Now What?

The immediate response after discovering a spouse's affair is commonly disbelief, anger, sadness, loss, or grief. It can take several years before the betrayed spouse is ready to even consider forgiveness, even if the partner who cheated begs for it. And though the cheating partner may immediately feel remorse and repeat "I'm sorry" over and over again, that apology may not get past the betrayed partner's outer layers of hurt.

Do You Need to Forgive?

Rebuilding after an affair—if that's what you choose to do—doesn't necessarily mean forgiving. Forgiveness implies that you must now trust your partner's promises. The promise "I'll never do it again, I will make up for it, I know I was wrong, and I won't let it happen again" may sound great in the beginning, but asking for forgiveness is actually putting all of the responsibility to forgive on the betrayed partner. Forgiveness, if it happens, is much more complex than this and, to a certain extent, isn't even under the control of the betrayed partner.

Try not to worry too much in the beginning about forgiveness. That will come in time. This book will discuss ways to move on from the affair, and to learn and grow from it, whether or not you are able to fully forgive your cheating partner right now or ever.

Forgiveness, as you know it now, may mean something totally different by the time you are done with this book. Forgiveness is a natural process that comes with a new awareness and understanding of your partner. Yet, even more important, you may have to forgive yourself first in order to move on.

For now, try not to make any major decisions about the relationship. In the initial phases of finding out about the affair, your emotions will be so unstable that it will be hard to know what you really want for your future. There is work to be done in deciding whether to stay or go, and some major shifts in insight have to happen before you can create a new vision of your relationship going forward.

It makes sense that you are not sure what you want; that is normal and healthy for this early phase of affair recovery. Let your focus right now be on ensuring that you are safe, that your children are safe, and that your basic needs are taken care of. Make sure you have shelter and food, and find support if you can. Support networks may be available in your community if you don't have family or friends in your area. Find a therapist to help you process the intense emotions that come up at this difficult time in your life.

Don't underestimate this crisis in your relationship. Both of you are experiencing a crisis. Crisis is an opportunity for change, but change is hard. Take care of yourself during this time, and be gentle while you and your loved ones are going through this early phase of affair recovery.

As you move through the later stages of affair recovery, your feelings will change, and you will move out of the crisis. This book will show you how.

The Role of Grief

A grieving process is normal after an affair. As you move through the grieving process, many emotions will emerge, possibly including anger, fear, denial, and eventually acceptance. You can feel as if you are grieving a death, and in many ways, you are. You are grieving the death of the old vision of your marriage or relationship. This is true whether you decide to stay together or move on.

Both partners must grieve their losses if they are to build a new marriage. Grief is triggered by the loss of the future you thought you were headed toward together. Whatever ideas you had about how you would grow old as a couple, retire, have grandchildren, rock on the front porch together, or travel the world, the affair has now challenged that vision of a shared future. Grief is a process of letting go of that vision. And, interestingly, grief has a way of making room for a different future if you choose to create that possibility going forward.

Initially after infidelity, it can be difficult for you to envision this new, shared future. The one person you turned to in the past for support when you were in pain is now the person causing you pain. It can seem as if there's no one to turn to. You may now think of your relationship as a liability instead of your strength. You may feel lonely and confused. You may long for the partner who always served as the support system in your life, and that time of innocence before you discovered the affair.

There is a time lapse in the grief process. The person who had the affair has known about the infidelity ever since it began. If you are just now discovering the affair, you are at a totally different point in the process than your partner is. You have only begun to feel your feelings about it, whereas your partner went through a myriad of her own emotions as the affair unfolded. You have some catching up to do.

Disclosure vs. Discovery

How you found out about the affair will largely determine how the grief process plays out. If your partner disclosed the infidelity, it can be a painful shock, but for some, this is better than discovering the affair yourself. If your partner confessed, it means he decided to no longer keep the affair a secret. It is the secret that can be the defining experience of betrayal.

For some, finding out about a hidden affair is a tough blow. Finding an e-mail or a hotel receipt, or hearing a phone message that wasn't meant for your ears can generate anger and confusion. Knowing that your partner had an affair, yet kept the affair from you, may be an even greater betrayal than the emotional or sexual relationship.

The reality will seem bleak initially. You can never go back to the old marriage; the vision you held of your life together is over.

Moving beyond an affair may mean that the old marriage has to end. Wherever you were headed in your past has led you to this point, and the thought of squeezing back into that relationship may feel almost impossible—and it is. If you try to go back to what was, you will only end up here again. That marriage, your "old" monogamy, led you to this point. But there can be many marriages within your lifetime—and all to the same partner. If this marriage is over, it may mean that there's another marriage waiting for you with the same spouse. If you are ready, this book can tell you how to move into a new marriage, together.

Moving Past Blame

If both partners are willing and ready to move into healing, you will notice a shift happening. Instead of feeling polarized into the good spouse and the bad spouse, the two of you will begin to realize that you each share responsibility for what happened in your relationship before the affair. There was most probably a dynamic in your marriage that contributed to the affair. When you start becoming aware of this shared dynamic, the recovery process becomes a shared experience between the two of you. The affair may even eventually move from being "his affair" or "her affair" to being "our affair."

When you start to feel this shift, it means you are moving into the next stage of your affair recovery. You are moving from the crisis phase into the understanding phase, where you are ready to look at what the affair meant to both of you.

The Phases of Recovery

I have identified three distinct phases of recovery from an affair: the crisis phase, the understanding (or insight) phase, and the vision phase.

The Crisis Phase

The first phase of affair recovery, the *crisis* phase, is now coming to an end. The initial shock and deep betrayal has played out, and enough of the chaos has slowed down for you to see that there was a relationship happening between you before the affair ever happened. And that relationship involved both of you.

The Understanding (or Insight) Phase

The second phase of affair recovery is the *understanding* (or *insight*) phase, and you are beginning to enter that phase when you start to look at *how* the affair happened. This second phase of affair recovery comes after the crisis has ebbed and you are moving past your intense anger and confusion. Although it can be a difficult time, this phase will help you experience empathy for each other and will give you hope for the future. You may still not know whether you want to make things work for the long run, but you will be able to do some of the work on your past to find out.

Understanding the affair and how it happened will be addressed in chapter 2. You will get clearer about what led you both to this point in your lives, and you will each explore the meaning of the affair. During this second phase of affair recovery, you may begin to wonder where your responsibility lies for what happened in your relationship. This is not about assigning blame to either of you, but you will deconstruct the affair and the history of your marriage to find out where the roots of the infidelity began. Starting to understand the affair can answer many of the questions that you may feel were left unanswered. Some of your frustration may be relieved at that point, and you may be ready to make some decisions about your relationship going forward.

The Vision Phase

When you reach the third phase of affair recovery, the *vision* phase, you will be able to create a new future together. You will be clear about what your new monogamy looks like, and the later chapters in this book will give you distinct steps for developing that new relationship, together.

The Six Steps of Recovery

There are also six steps that will help you move through the after-shocks of the affair so that you can recover your equilibrium as a couple.

Step 1: Take care of yourself. If you are in the crisis phase, if you just found out about your partner's affair, it's normal to feel distraught. You may be overwhelmed and in shock. It's important to take care of yourself at this time. Even if you have a family to care for, your needs must come first now. Remember, you can't pour from an empty pitcher. Take care of yourself during this phase by letting yourself feel your feelings, getting sufficient rest and nutrition, and finding a support system. You may want to do additional self-care, like massage, acupuncture, or yoga. Think of friends you can call whenever you need to talk. Being alone in your pain can make it harder. Find an online group of helpful, nonjudgmental people to help support you right now.

Step 2: Communicate. Learning to communicate can be difficult, and if your style or skills at dealing with conflict before the affair weren't great, they are probably not helping you now. The skills you will learn in this book will give you a good framework for communicating within your relationship. You will need to carve out some time to practice your new communication skills, and you may need a therapist to help you do that. Or you can use the exercises in this book to practice a new kind of dialogue about your feelings and needs with your partner.

Step 3: Have a date night. If you choose to stay together, set aside one night a week just for you and your partner. This is time that is separate from therapy and the children. You may feel awkward at first, as if you were dating, just as you did in the beginning of your relationship. But you need this time to explore your new relationship together. On your date, find something other than the affair to talk about. Give each other a break on date night by keeping things light and polite. Even if you are feeling intense emotions, you may need a break from the constant worry and frustration.

Step 4: Address the reality. Why did the affair happen? Through insight and discussion, you will explore together how you got to this place. Now that you are taking care of yourself, practicing your communication skills, and setting aside time to be together, you can begin the real work of figuring out how you both created the path you are now on. Only one of you may have cheated, but both of you need to change now if you are to stay together. In what ways can each of you grow from this experience?

Step 5: Create a new monogamy agreement. Your new monogamy agreement will clear away all the unspoken expectations that led to the betrayal and hurt that you feel now. You can rewrite your agreement to include anything that the two of you may find valuable for your future. This new vision of your relationship going forward is a new beginning. It's not a way to go back to your old relationship, but rather a way to create a new partnership based on a mutual understanding of what will work for both of you.

Step 6: Initiate erotic recovery. Spending a lifetime together and staying monogamous won't be easy. Let's face it: desiring one person for a lifetime doesn't happen effortlessly. It happens because you apply the energy and practice it. Monogamy isn't something that happens automatically because you made a vow when you first committed to each other. Monogamy is a practice. You must focus on it, honor it, and choose it every day. Working every day on your erotic life means that you are both committing to that practice. And as with anything that you need to practice, some days will go better than others. Eventually you will get better at it, until one day you may even find that you are monogamy experts.

More Than One Marriage… to the Same Person

Again, you can have more than one marriage in your lifetime—all to the same person. One marriage may be strictly about young love and *limerence*: that feeling of being in love and in lust with your partner. Another marriage within your marriage may be purely about having and raising children, if you choose to do so. As the children move on, you may find a new level of companionship between you and your spouse that feels like a whole new experience of couplehood. Later you may find that aging together gives you a new experience of love and caring that deepens your bond in unique and important ways.

After an affair, many couples actually find it comforting to know that they don't have to go back to their old relationships. After an affair, as traumatic as it may be, you and your spouse have the opportunity to usher in a new marriage between the two of you.

This rebuilding or starting over can restore hope. The hopelessness resulting from infidelity comes from the initial realization that there truly is no hope for that old marriage. That old marriage ended with the affair. However, this may mean that another door has opened for you both to create a new partnership, this time with your old spouses. This new marriage and new monogamy can be the ideal relationship you have been looking for.

Affairs as Self-Growth

An affair can happen when the relationship is stuck in its growth pattern and needs something to get it moving again. If you are looking back and wondering *How was our relationship stuck before this happened?* or *Where did we need to grow before this affair shook our foundations?* a good first step is to examine what has happened as a result of the affair. How have you both changed since it was disclosed?

Whenever frustration emerges in a relationship, it means that someone is trying to grow. One or both partners, when frustrated, feel pressure to make a change. To stay healthy and rewarding, relationships need to always be growing and changing. Like all of life, growth equals expansion and health. Relationships need to keep up with the changing developmental needs of each partner, or they get stuck. To help your relationship grow to its full potential, an affair may push both of you to make much-needed changes in the relationship.

One couple described it like this:

"Before the affair, we were in our own little bubbles," said Tom of his marriage to Madeline. "We never saw much importance in sharing our days or our deeper feelings. We each had a role to play: Maddy was the good wife, and I was the good husband. She cooked and cleaned, and ran our children around, and I worked; in fact I worked all the time. That was what I was taught to do. Isn't that what a good husband should do?"

"But," Madeline added, "we never talked about what was happening in our emotional relationship. We rarely had sex anymore, and I felt trapped at home. Tom felt stuck in a job he hated, because he was trying to be a good provider. I had no idea."

"Since the affair," Tom continued, "it has become clear to both of us that we had just stopped talking, probably years ago, maybe even before the kids were born. It's almost as if the affair crept in under the fault lines of our emotional life. I think we needed it to happen in order to wake up and pay attention. I think we never would have made it if we had kept going in that direction. Eventually we would have divorced. The affair was this shock to our systems, but it showed us a clear direction about where we needed to work on our marriage if we were ever going to make this happen."

Both Tom and Madeline had ignored a deeper awareness of their inability to communicate. The affair then created an opening, through the pain it caused, for them to work on new ways to talk to each other about their feelings. It took an earthquake of grand proportions in their relationship to turn their marriage in the direction of what they both desired: real emotional intimacy.

The Role of Empathy in Affair Recovery

Empathy is the capacity to experience the feelings of someone else, to put yourself in the other person's emotional shoes. Part of healing from the affair will mean working at understanding why it happened, which, as noted in the introduction, may or may not be because your partner was unhappy in your marriage.

Why did the affair happen? What made your partner look for or pursue outside opportunities for sex or affection? You don't have to agree with what your partner did, but if you can come to a place of understanding *why* she did it, you may be able to develop some empathy, and then you can decide where to go from there. The normal anger, rage, disbelief, and lack of understanding that naturally follow the discovery of an affair won't help when it comes time to make major decisions about your relationship. As you work through this book, you and your partner will talk a lot about the affair, about why she did it and how it affected you.

Empathy means that if you put yourself in your partner's shoes, you may begin to feel what she was feeling, which will help you understand why the affair happened. This doesn't mean that you need to forgive your partner's behavior, only that you understand what she *felt* at the time.

And it works both ways: only when your partner can feel empathy for *you* will she be able to take full responsibility for the affair. When she truly feels your pain, only then will she feel authentic regret, which differs from selfish regret caused by guilt and remorse. Guilt causes the betraying partner internal pain; that's about her. It is when she feels true empathy that she will experience genuine regret at causing you pain. She can only begin to make changes that can salvage your relationship when she feels real empathy.

What Is the New Monogamy?

The new monogamy is a new way of looking at marriage and committed relationships. Most of us have followed a path to commitment that was provided for us by our culture and upbringing. We were taught what a committed relationship should look like, and we assumed that this was the only way to have a real partnership.

You may have had a vision since you were young of getting married. You fantasized about being with a certain type of person, committing to that person in a certain way, and having all of the trappings and ceremony of that explicit monogamy commitment. You may have dreamed of the perfect wedding dress or the most romantic vows. Perhaps you wanted to marry in the church or synagogue you grew up in because it had meaning for you, your family, or your community. You took vows that were based on promises that you were told were your religious beliefs and globally shared values.

The Fairy Tale

But you may have engaged in these culturally defined rituals without truly looking at your own personal beliefs, your needs in the relationship, and what you wanted out of it. You may have only briefly discussed each other's needs and expectations. After a lifetime of reading fairy tales, watching romantic movies, and seeing your family members practicing these rituals, you moved blindly and happily into monogamy. You may have assumed, wrongly, that all it would take to be blissful was to find a person who would commit to you, one you could trust. You thought you could then move on happily with your life, without giving much thought to your real relationship needs. Riding off into the sunset, you thought you were set for life.

Often, affairs happen because one or both partners, as Tom and Madeline found, are operating on autopilot. One or both partners have needs that may initially be seen as unimportant. If those needs go unmet, they may get met elsewhere. Often this happens when one or both partners expect that the institution of marriage—or the explicit monogamy agreement in which each partner verbally or ritually commits to one another—is enough to guarantee fidelity. Saying "I do" does not guarantee fidelity. It is not enough. It's only the beginning.

When you committed to your partner, you both came to the relationship with certain expectations about what it would be like. You may have discussed some of these agreements with your partner, for example, where you would live, your work and financial arrangements, or when you might have children. These were your *explicit monogamy agreements*.

Yet you also have many expectations that you may never have talked about, but which you hold your partner to, and vice versa. These are *implicit monogamy agreements*, and they are often the ones that are operating all the time, even when you don't realize it. When your relationship is troubled and a partner cheats, these implicit agreements are the misunderstandings that trip you up.

Some examples of breached implicit agreements are "I thought we could have close friends of the opposite sex, and it would be no big deal even after we were married" or "I didn't realize that having my ex-lover connect with me on the computer would bother you."

After an affair, couples struggle with the realization that their marriages weren't as they had thought. These implicit understandings (or misunderstandings) must now become explicit. Couples who choose to stay together after infidelity have the chance to create new, explicit agreements about what can and can't happen in their marriages, based on each couple's needs and desires, and what's realistically manageable for both partners, not on what society at large thinks is healthy and right for them.

The new monogamy can be described as the conscious choices a couple makes about their sexual and emotional fidelity when they both agree to stay together and make it work. The new monogamy also means that each marriage is highly individualized. Partners have the right to make any agreement they want that works for both of them concerning what their monogamy will look like. As you'll see, this may or may not include sustaining and revisiting the old rules of their original vows. Or it could mean making agreements that aren't considered acceptable in most marriage traditions. In the new monogamy, both partners get to agree on what their relationship will look like, based solely on their shared needs, expectations, and desires.

Implicit Misunderstandings at the Root of the Affair

As mentioned, when we marry or commit to a life partner, we often assume that we understand the rules we are agreeing to. Most of us don't bother to explore what marriage or commitment truly means to us underneath our cultural and social assumptions and expectations, and what kinds of beliefs we are bringing to our marriages.

Implicit monogamy agreements may include assumptions like "You'll never be attracted to another person besides me" or "Neither of us will ever be interested in sex or emotional connection with another person." If we're really honest with ourselves, these implicit agreements may include "We promise to be faithful at least until one of us grows tired of the other," "I know you won't cheat, but I probably will," "I'll be faithful, but you won't because you're a guy" (traditionally a woman's belief), or "We'll be faithful except for a little swinging when we go on vacation."

Some implicit assumptions are more damaging to a relationship than others.

One night, Ellen was looking in the glove box of her husband's car, searching for a street map. She stumbled upon a receipt for a night in a local hotel, and sat in the car for an hour, shocked. She didn't know what to do with her feelings; she was devastated. She walked slowly back to the house and confronted Sam with the receipt. He was initially taken aback but then came clean about it: "I was really tired from working and felt totally stressed. I just started to crave a warm body. I hired a girl to come, well, take care of me."

Ellen was shocked. "You went to a hooker!"

"Well, yeah, don't worry, we used a condom. It was just for stress relief. It didn't mean anything. Is that a big deal? I mean, honey, it was only sex—I swear."

For Sam, hiring a prostitute was just something men did occasionally. During a father-son fishing trip when Sam was fifteen, his own father had discussed it with him, letting him know that if he wanted to lose his virginity, his dad would find him a "nice, clean professional girl." The men in his family had always talked about their visits to sex workers when their partners weren't around. It was considered normal and healthy in his family, but not something you talked about with the women.

For Ellen, going to a prostitute was the epitome of dishonesty and the ultimate betrayal. She felt hurt and embarrassed. She hadn't realized that in Sam's mind, it was part of their implicit monogamy agreement that he would occasionally pay for sex outside of the marriage.

Implicit agreements can cause problems in relationships if each partner has a separate version of what monogamy means. For example, if one partner thinks dirty dancing and rubbing against strangers in a club is acceptable but his spouse considers that cheating, they will likely experience conflict.

For some, going to a bachelor party with a female stripper may feel "normal" and nonthreatening. But if this implicit understanding isn't discussed, it can feel like a betrayal to a wife who doesn't quite agree and wasn't consulted before the party.

It's important to understand the distinctions between explicit and implicit agreements, because the conflict between the two can be at the root of an affair. The conflict between you and your partner's explicit and implicit agreements will have to be dealt with if you are to move forward in your relationship. Part of moving into a new future with your spouse will be making your implicit agreements transparent and explicit.

The New Monogamy Agreement

New monogamy agreements (shortened hereafter in this book to "monogamy agreements") can be anything you and your partner decide is right for you. You may decide to keep your marriage exactly as it was, but to revisit and renegotiate your explicit agreements through the years to make sure you are both getting your needs met. Since the new monogamy is all about making implicit agreements explicit and helping you negotiate what you really, truly desire in your relationship, any agreement is fine as long as it works for both partners.

The next few chapters will discuss vital issues like trust, empathy, how to learn what the affair has to teach you, and exploring your existing explicit and implicit agreements, so that by the time you reach chapter 5, you will have worked toward healing from the affair and will be ready to negotiate a new agreement that works for both of you.

The Monogamy Continuum

In the new monogamy, monogamy is considered to be on a continuum from totally closed—meaning no sexual, sensual, or emotional connection with others outside of the marriage—to totally open, with both partners being allowed to fully explore sexual, sensual, and emotional connections with people besides the primary partner, while still making that partner the top priority (hence "monogamy"). The continuum may also include having physically or emotionally affectionate and bonded outside relationships without sex; sexual play with others if both partners are present; or total openness, where both partners are allowed unlimited sexual or emotional relationships with others.

Chapter 4 goes into specific "nontraditional" new monogamy agreements, but for now, let's discuss the process of forging your own new monogamy agreement.

Who Makes the Rules?

For any relationship to function without hurt or betrayal, there must be a structure for your commitment to each other so that you both understand the meaning of your relationship. This is normal for pair-bonding humans. Almost from the beginning of a relationship, couples begin to define and label their commitments to one another. This labeling creates safety for each person. They recognize what the boundaries are when there's a name for what they are doing. Just friends, hooking up, boyfriend, girlfriend, going out, dating, going steady, committed, engaged, married, married in an open relationship—these definitions all make clear what can and can't be done within and outside of the relationship. Yet you can't expect these labels to mean the same thing to everyone.

Both partners must be the primary rule setters of their relationship structure. Chapter 5 walks you through constructing a new monogamy agreement, which will entail you and your partner discussing your needs and desires for your relationship in detail, and creating an explicit agreement to use going forward into your new marriage. Each partner must have an equal voice in how the monogamy will work. You don't have to label your relationship at all if it makes you uncomfortable, or you can define it very clearly. But your new monogamy will have explicit boundaries and rules. This demands such a high level of honesty and transparency that it is antithetical to the dishonesty of infidelity.

Creating Rules about the Three Aspects of Infidelity

Remember, an affair consists of three parts: the outside emotional relationship, the dishonesty, and the sexual relationship. The rules of a new monogamy relationship address all of these three areas by maintaining honest communication about each agreement, and instituting a process of renegotiation if any of the agreements become unwieldy or no longer serve the relationship.

The first rule to make concerns those who are expanding their relationships in new ways, making the rules about outside emotional relationships important. Questions to consider include "Can we have friendships that are not shared?" "Do we have to tell each other every time we speak to a friend online?" "Should there be outside contact beyond a shared sexual encounter?" "Can either partner contact a sexual partner when we are not all together?"

The most important rule about dishonesty in your new monogamy relationship is this: there can't be any. A new monogamy relationship can work only if there are no secrets. For instance, deciding on a case-by-case basis that certain things don't need to be discussed in detail (for instance, private thoughts and feelings about someone else) establishes a privacy rule that is comfortable *at this time* for you as a couple. But even this rule must be readdressed from time to time to avoid any future misunderstandings. Call this your "privacy versus secrecy rule," and come back to it whenever you believe that something falls under this category and needs to be discussed. (If you don't like the word "rule," call it a "caveat" or an "issue," but find a way to come back to the things that will need to be discussed several times throughout the lifetime of your agreement.)

Your rules about sex must be addressed and discussed in detail. In chapter 5, you will discuss questions like "Should we tell each other when we masturbate, or is it private?" "Do we share our thoughts and fantasies, or keep them to ourselves?" "Can we look at pornography alone?" "How often do we have sex?" "Can we hug and kiss another person?" "Can we have sexual encounters with others when we are together?" "Can we ever have sex with other people, with permission?" "What about protection and birth control?" All of these questions will be addressed as you develop your new monogamy agreement in chapter 5.

Does the New Monogamy Mean Opening Your Marriage?

You may not want an open marriage. You may not want to have any sexual contact with people outside of your primary relationship. You may only be interested in redefining your commitment to your partner by drawing the new vision of your relationship in ways that define your new sex life and your new emotional connection. You now have more options than you may have ever considered before. Though you may feel shocked or dismayed at the thought of discussing opening or widening your marriage to include other partners, remember that these options are just that: optional. Your new monogamy will be of your own making, and both partners must fully agree to it.

The affair may have devastated your ideas and expectations of both your marriage and your partner. The good news is that you can save your marriage and develop a stronger, more intimate bond by creating a new agreement in which all of your wishes and desires for your marriage are on the table.

Successful relationships are the ones in which the partners have a solid foundation of emotional connection and feel secure in themselves. They feel strong together and believe in their commitment to each other. They believe that their priority is to commit to that special partner and that their relationship with each other comes first. They are able to negotiate their boundaries and stop any outside emotional connection or sexuality if it threatens their primary commitment. And they are able to communicate all of their desires, longings, fears, appreciations, and concerns to one another.

CHAPTER 2

Listening to the Affair

The aftershocks of the affair have probably not yet fully worn off. You may still be feeling angry, hurt, triggered, defensive, sad, betrayed, and very lonely. Yet by picking up this book, you've made the decision to work on your relationship. One of the things you'll need to do to help initiate the healing process is look at why the affair happened and even what it may have to teach you. As hard as it may be to contemplate right now, the affair may actually point directly to the parts of yourself that you will need to work on to grow as an individual, as well as the parts of the relationship that weren't working before the affair began.

What You Had Together Led You Here

Lots of couples have told me that an affair was the best thing that ever happened to them. This realization comes after the initial crisis has passed, when you begin to have insight into what led to the affair. It may be difficult to think about it this way, but for the couples I've worked with, healing began when they realized that the relationship could *only* have led to infidelity. Looking back, it seems that the affair, or a real marital crisis, was inevitable.

The partners realize then that their original monogamy agreement needs to be reexamined. Many couples find that the affair is a wake-up call to create a new and more vital partnership, one where excitement and intrigue are an inside job.

> Anne and Chris had been married for twenty years. They were one of those couples that realized that the affair might have been what they needed to save their marriage. "We *never* would have made it over the long haul if it hadn't been for Chris's affair. I know it sounds crazy," Anne said, "but I realized after I found out he was cheating that I had to change—and fast—if I wanted to make our marriage work. It wasn't just Chris who had drifted; I was so far out of the marriage that it was no surprise that this was where it led. One of us was bound to cheat eventually. I was never home, and when I was, I was texting or on the computer with my friends. And we never talked. I had shut him out, and I'm not even sure why. He tried for a long time to get close to me. I think I was so unhappy that I didn't know how to reach out and make it work. I couldn't talk about my feelings with him, so I didn't even try. And finally he gave up and found someone else to talk to. Well, that woke me the hell up. I was shocked but not really surprised; does that make sense?
>
> "Now we are talking more, spending more time together, and making room in our lives for our intimate needs. I know it was his choice to go outside the marriage. I'm not saying he did the right thing. It hurt. But I'm almost glad this happened. We had drifted so far apart that eventually, we would have just broken up. Now we are really working on things. We are choosing to stay together and make things work. We are the lucky ones."

Sometimes, an affair can be a shock to the system that can bring a faltering marriage back to life. The only way to take advantage of this shocking revelation, however, is to look at what the affair is trying to tell you, and to go through the steps to recovery and to a new monogamy agreement.

How and Why Did the Affair Happen?

Often, when we discover that a partner has been cheating, the first question is an anguished "Why?" This often-unanswerable question is what drives us to ruminate on what happened, and we may force our partners to talk about the details over and over again, hoping to find the answers we are searching for. If our relationships seemed fine before we found out about the affair, the "why" can plague us, make us lose sleep, and keep us from being able to focus on other tasks.

One of the first things you will need to do to heal from the affair is explore this question of why it happened and be open to hearing the real, honest truth. Most people want to blame the cheating partner. And the cheating partner does have to take responsibility for pursuing the outside relationship. But no affair happens in a vacuum. So, part of asking "why" will most likely include the betrayed partner hearing things about her own behaviors that she may not want to hear, such as ways that she exited the relationship prior to the affair, perhaps without even realizing it.

Collusion in the Affair

Collusion means "secret cooperation." The dictionary says that collusion is "secret cooperation between two people in order to do something underhanded or undesirable" (*Microsoft Encarta College Dictionary*, 1st ed., s.v. "collusion"). Many couples, if they are honest with themselves, may find that the partner who was cheated on colluded with the infidelity even if he didn't participate directly in the affair. That means that on some level, there was some type of cooperation, even if unconscious, to make the affair happen.

This secret cooperation may mean the betrayed partner is doing something in the relationship to collude with his partner's behavior, even if he doesn't realize it. This can be difficult to hear and even harder to figure out. Interestingly, Israel Charny and Sivan Parnass (1995) found that 89 percent of betrayed spouses were either unconsciously aware of their partners' infidelity or were in collusion with them, even if they claimed to be opposed to the affair.

To be unconsciously aware means that on some level, the betrayed partner had an idea that his spouse was cheating. Maybe it was a passing thought or a hunch. It may not have been even a fully formed suspicion. But most of the spouses in the study admitted that they knew on some level that the affair was going on. It may be that in retrospect, it's easier to notice the signs. Or it may be that we sense betrayal in our relationships even if we don't always know what's actually happening.

> Maria and Frank had been stuck in conflict over Maria's affair for over a year. Maria had cheated on Frank with a neighbor, Joe, someone they saw weekly for card games and occasional barbecues. When Frank found out that Maria had cheated with Joe, he became incensed and almost left her, threatening to take all of their money and fight her in court for full custody of their children.
>
> As time progressed and Maria and Frank discussed the affair, Maria shared her confusion with her husband: "I always felt that you approved of my relationship with Joe. You saw how he flirted with me, and you even encouraged me to go over there when his wife was out of town. You used to say that Joe was probably lonely and that maybe I should go over and have a drink with him. Now you are so mad at me! There's some kind of mixed message here."
>
> Frank was furious with Maria for insinuating that he pushed her into the affair: "I never told you to cheat with

him. Did I ever say, 'Go sleep with Joe; he and his wife aren't having any'?"

As Frank's feelings calmed down, he tried to see things from Maria's point of view, to find some empathy for her experience: "I guess it makes sense that she would move toward Joe. I do remember thinking that Joe really needed affection, and I know Maria can be very sweet. Frankly, I was so busy with my work, and—well, to be honest— maybe I did push them together. Maybe I was hoping that they would cheat so I would have an excuse to leave. I might have unconsciously pushed them together so I could blame Maria for ending our marriage. I could maybe then feel kind of self-righteous about the whole thing. I am so embarrassed to admit that this might have been partly my fault."

Maria said, "This is not your fault. I definitely made the move to step over the line. But we were on a slippery slope. And I very much appreciate your admitting that you pushed Joe and me together."

By admitting that he had played a part in his wife's affair, Frank realized he had unconsciously colluded with her about the affair. He had participated in the infidelity by actively setting up the scenario where Joe and Maria would begin a sexual affair and then turning the other way when he suspected they were cheating.

If Frank had not been able to admit his part in the affair, they could have ended their marriage, and he could have held on to his role as the victim, accusing Maria of breaking their monogamy agreement. It was almost as if he had created a new form of monogamy in which she would have an outside relationship so that he could live in denial.

Affairs as Exits

An *exit* can be any behavior that a partner uses to avoid being truly present in the relationship, whether emotionally, psychologically, sexually, or even physically. Harville Hendrix (2008), author of the best-selling self-help book *Getting the Love You Want: A Guide for Couples*, says smaller exits can include anything that helps you avoid dealing with conflict or intimacy, including overfocusing on the children, being on the computer, checking e-mails, texting, cleaning the house, staying late at work, or even playing golf. Any behavior that is used to avoid ways to engage with your partner is considered an exit. Bigger exits include things like gambling, drinking, and taking drugs. An affair is considered one of the biggest exits and is called "an invisible divorce" (ibid.).

Affairs are only one way to exit from the relationship, but they can be a powerful and damaging way to avoid the intimacy of a monogamous partnership. However, whenever the person who is exiting traces her behavior back to the moment she exited, it often becomes clear that at that time, her partner was exiting as well. If the cheating partner can trace her behavior back to the point where the indiscretion began, it may become clear that the affair was an attempt to deal with the feelings of a partner who "exited" the relationship first.

> Mike and Sheila came to therapy after Mike had an affair
> with a woman he met on the Internet. He had been coming
> home from work every night tired and distant from Sheila.
> Sheila was very rarely in the house when he got home,
> and he ate dinner alone most evenings. Every time he
> tried to talk to Sheila about his loneliness and feelings
> of disconnection, she would get defensive and accuse
> Mike of trying to shut down her needs professionally.

"I would ask Mike if he really wanted me to quit my job," she said, "and I let him know that this really made me angry. He would deny that this was what he wanted, and get quiet and withdraw from me. He would go on the computer for the rest of the night, and frankly, I felt relieved whenever he stopped bugging me."

Mike said, "I never wanted her to stop working. I wanted her to be home with me. And I wouldn't have minded if she worked a couple of nights and then came home to be with me. But even when she was home, she always seemed to be thinking about work, not me. Every time I tried to talk to her about it, we would end up in the same old argument. What was the point? Eventually I started a relationship with this woman who advertised on adult websites. She never let me down, and whenever I was lonely, she was there for me. Of course, I had to pay her, but I felt that she really listened to me when I talked. It didn't matter whether she really cared; what mattered was that she was there."

Often, one or both partners may see an affair as a way to avoid conflict or intimacy, and eventually may see it as an exit from the relationship. In exploring why your partner pursued an affair, you may discover that he perceived that you exited the relationship first. This can be a difficult thing to accept, especially amid the fresh pain of a newly discovered affair. Yet, if you are both courageous enough to face such difficult truths, these revelations can be healing and can ultimately bring you both closer together. It may even make you closer than you were prior to the affair.

The rest of this chapter will help you explore why the affair happened, including the exits you and your partner may have used to avoid intimacy or conflict, or to cover up a distance that was growing between you.

The Affair as a Catalyst for Positive Change

The discovery of an affair can spark a crisis that can lead to a break in a pattern of negative interactions, such as exiting behaviors. There may be other negative coping strategies that you and your partner have used to avoid talking about uncomfortable subjects. Some couples avoid conflict by exiting, and others avoid the real issues they want to discuss by camouflaging them with other things. They may talk about the children or work, for instance, when they really want to talk about the marriage. Or they may talk about money when they really want to talk about sex. What ways do you avoid the conflict in your relationship? An affair may be a way to break you out of some of these old coping strategies.

Couples who have experienced affairs are forced into new discussions about former unmet needs that lead to new and creative ways of moving forward and staying together. Changing the old methods of communication can lead to communication about how to make monogamy and commitment work in a new erotic and emotional relationship. When couples focus on how they can learn from experiencing an affair, sometimes each partner grows as an individual.

Mike and Sheila had to go through their affair to realize that the way they communicated ended up shutting both of them down. Neither got the need for connection met in the old relationship, and the more they tried to talk about it, the worse their communication became. Sheila saw Mike as needy and dependent, looking to her for attention, when she really wanted to be focused on her work. Although her work took her out of the house and she thought he was upset about her job, Mike really was longing for connection. Mike perceived Sheila as stonewalling and defensive every time he tried to talk about his loneliness. Instead of pursuing her and explaining what he longed for, he retreated and went on the computer, looking to get his needs met outside of the relationship instead of working harder to be heard.

Neither of them was able to communicate to one another in a way that the other could hear, so they just ended up going around and around, caught in the same arguments. They each felt the same way they always had when they had tried to express themselves. This frustration always led to a feeling of being unheard and not seen by one another.

After Mike's online affair, they both realized that the way they talked about their needs triggered each other's defensiveness. When the topic of Mike's needs came up, Sheila went into survival mode, attacking Mike to defend against her own feelings of inadequacy. Mike would feel her attack, want to avoid the conflict, and then do what he knew best: flee, either by shutting down emotionally, literally leaving the room, or going on the computer.

This fight-or-flight response got triggered because both of them were afraid: Mike of never having his need for connection met, and Sheila of being consumed by Mike's needs. Because Mike and Sheila kept reacting in old, ingrained ways to one another's attempts to be heard, they were trapped in a cycle of conflict that eventually led Mike to reach out to a woman online to meet his emotional needs.

Sheila realized she needed to change the way she reacted to Mike. In this way she could learn to grow and change, and regardless of what happened in their relationship, she could become a stronger and more adaptable person. She recognized that her coping skills were unhealthy for her and unhelpful in her own life. She would get angry, and feel alone and frustrated by herself, separated from Mike. She wasn't getting her emotional needs met in the end anyway.

After the affair, they knew things had to change. They began to recognize their fight-or-flight pattern, or their pursue-and-distance relationship, and started to try some new behaviors. Sheila forced herself to stay present when Mike was upset about something, and learned to talk to him instead of leaving as soon as he expressed an emotion or need that made her feel uncomfortable. Mike began to feel seen and heard in a new way, and no longer felt that Sheila was abandoning him or running away. He stopped leaving as soon as he felt conflict, and pushed himself to stay present and talk to Sheila about his feelings. As the communication style between them changed, their whole way of being in a relationship changed.

New Ways to Communicate

As you explore what happens in your own relationship later in this chapter, you'll need to become familiar with some new communication techniques that will help derail your normal, defensive ways of responding to one another. These techniques are at the core of many of the tools in this book, and will serve you for the rest of your life, not only in your marriage, but also in all of your relationships. If you learn how to use these techniques well, you will discover that you have become a better listener to your partner and everyone else in your life, and you will also get better at speaking your feelings.

The dialogue process you will learn is from Imago Relationship Therapy, developed by Harville Hendrix (2008), and is adapted with permission. There are three important aspects of this dialogue process: mirroring, validating, and empathizing, and we will review them many times throughout this book. You will use these first three communication techniques when you are listening to your partner or your partner is listening to you.

A fourth helpful communication technique is the use of "I" statements. All four of these techniques work to help take the blaming language out of a conversation while including language that makes both people feel heard and understood.

Mirroring

The first aspect of the Imago dialogue process is called *mirroring*, which simply means that you reflect back to the speaker what you heard her say. For example, if your partner says, "I'm afraid to let you know about one of my sexual fantasies because you might judge me," you would merely respond to what you heard her say, and try not to express a judgment about it. This would sound like "You're afraid that if you let me know about one of your sexual fantasies, I will judge you." Mirroring makes the speaker feel seen and heard rather than judged or criticized, and gives space for the dialogue to happen. It also allows the listener some time to listen and hear what the speaker has to say without having to immediately think of a retort.

Validating

The second important technique is *validation*. Validation means that the listener makes the speaker feel that her experience or actions are understandable. Examples of validation are "Yes, I can understand how you would act that way, knowing what I know about you," and "I can see how that statement I made might have made you react that way." By validating the speaker's experience, you once again defuse the defensiveness. Most of us get defensive when we think that someone else is implying that we shouldn't have done something or that we shouldn't feel what we feel.

One common example that I see in couples is the tendency to try to comfort someone by telling her to stop feeling pain. Although well intentioned, telling someone "Don't cry" is not very validating. "It makes sense that you're sad right now" is a more validating statement that lets the person have her emotions. This also avoids making her feel ashamed for crying.

By using validation, even if you disagree with your partner or don't think that she should feel a certain way or that she should have done a certain behavior, you can still find a way to understand her experience. Validation doesn't mean you agree or approve. Expressing validation is a powerful way to make the speaker feel seen and understood.

When Mike and Sheila started talking, Mike was able to express to her that sometimes her coming home late reminded him of his childhood. It brought up old feelings of not being important to someone he loved. He shared with her that when he was young, his dad would come home, often drunk, and ignore Mike's attempts to get his attention. Sheila's focus on work reminded him of his dad and brought up that old sense of feeling unloved as a child.

When Sheila heard this, she suddenly understood why Mike felt so abandoned by her. Her late work hours all of a sudden meant something totally different to her, and she could see, from his perspective, why he was always accusing her of purposely choosing to abandon him by staying out late.

She validated his experience by responding, "Oh, it never even occurred to me that this was what you were feeling. I thought you were just being selfish in telling me not to work late. But now I can see perfectly why it's been so hard for you, considering what you went through with your dad. This makes perfect sense now. I'm so glad you told me."

Empathizing

By *empathizing*, the listener expresses that he understands or is attempting to understand his partner's feelings in the situation. The difference between empathy and validation is that by validating your partner, you are expressing an understanding of *why* he might have done what he did, and with empathy, you are attempting to actually *feel* what he might have felt in that situation.

Sheila told Mike that she often felt stressed when she came home from work. Having him confront her right away when she came in the door and accuse her of doing something wrong always made her feel more stressed, as well as incompetent as a wife. Mike empathized, even though it hadn't been his intent to make her feel that way. When he looked at the situation from her perspective, he was able to understand how she might have felt pressured and criticized by his approach, and by tapping into his own experiences of feeling pressured and criticized, he gained a powerful insight into how she had felt during those late-night confrontations. Though his needs were entirely valid, his way of expressing them put Sheila on the spot, and by using empathy, he could understand better why it had been hard for her to respond to him in the way that he wanted her to. He was able to say, "Wow, I understand how that must have felt. You must have felt so much pressure when you came home. I've had people attack me when I've come through the door too; that's not at all what I wanted to do to you!"

With validation and empathy, you are not required to condone or agree with anything your partner says, only to do your best to understand his experiences and feelings, and to communicate that understanding to him. Even if this is difficult, remember that having empathy for your partner is the first step in beginning to heal from the affair and in rebuilding mutual trust. If you really are having a hard time coming to a place of understanding, find some part of your partner's experience that does make sense to you and try to validate and empathize with that piece only.

> Mike accused Sheila of having her own affair when she came home late one night and was on her smartphone checking her messages as she walked in the door. "So, you are talking to your boyfriend before you even take off your coat?" he said. Sheila tried not to respond with defensiveness, but to understand where he might be coming from: "Mike, it makes sense that you might be upset with me for coming home late. And here I am still working even as I walk in the door. I imagine you are anxious to see me and get our evening started. It sounds like you are upset. Can we sit and talk for a moment?"
>
> Validating and empathizing with Mike didn't mean that Sheila had to address Mike's accusation that she was having an affair. That part didn't make sense to her. But she did understand that he might be angry or frustrated that even as she walked in the door, she was still working and that he was expressing his feelings in the only way he could in that moment. It didn't make it right, and she didn't have to agree to it or get into an argument. But validating him actually helped Mike back off from his anger, and he was able to calm down so that they then could talk out what was happening between them without repeating old patterns.

The idea is to let your partner know that you understand things from his perspective, not that you have to agree with him. For example, if you could travel across an imaginary bridge to your partner's side of an imaginary planet, and really crawl inside of his experience for a moment, what would it feel like? That's what validation is:

a way to express to your partner that you understand what it feels like to be on his planet, even if it's a totally different experience on your side of the bridge. On your side of the planet, you think differently, see the world differently, and feel different feelings, so you probably won't agree and won't have the same emotions as your partner. That doesn't mean you can't understand where your partner is coming from, knowing him, his personality, and his past as you do. And as you learn to communicate and understand each other's experiences in deeper and more meaningful ways, you will be able to empathize and validate even more often and in more meaningful ways.

Using "I" Statements

Using "I" *statements* is a way to take any blame out of your conversation, by taking responsibility for your own feelings and reactions rather than blaming your partner for them. With "I" statements, you refrain from telling your partner that she did something to make you feel a certain way or that she is responsible for making you react in a certain way. You take full responsibility for your own reactions and behaviors.

> When Jim and Jenna were in my office struggling with the aftermath of Jenna's affair, I coached both of them to respond to one another with "I" statements. Jenna told Jim, "I felt taken for granted, taking care of the kids and the house all the time while I thought you were working to support us. That's why I turned to Bob in the first place."
>
> Jenna could have said, "You made me feel taken for granted," but with this "I" statement, she owned her own feelings without explicitly blaming Jim. Jim was able to tell Jenna, "I felt lonely when I sensed that distance from you." In this way, both were able to express their emotional experiences without spiraling into conflict with accusations and counteraccusations.

"I" statements typically take the form of "I feel/felt
_____ when _____," with the last half of
the statement being something that your partner has said or done—
for example, "I felt angry when you told me you were taking a business trip, when you were really with your mistress" or "I feel anxious
when you tell me how you met the man you've been sleeping with."
Notice that both of these statements clearly state the speaker's feelings and the behavior or words that are at the root of those feelings,
but they don't blame the other person for the speaker's feelings.

Use "I" statements when you are discussing your feelings with
your partner. They will help keep you both from getting defensive
and angry while you talk about why the affair happened.

Using the Imago Dialogue

The Imago dialogue process is simple. One person is the sender
(the speaker), and the other is the receiver (the listener.) Before you
and your partner engage in any of the dialogues in this book, choose
who will be the sender and who will be the receiver. You will switch
for each dialogue so that both of you will get a chance to take on
each role.

The sender's job is to be as honest, yet as kind and compassion-
ate, as possible. The goal of these dialogues is always to get to the
heart of the issues that you are struggling with as a couple.

In most of your past conversations, both of you have probably
concentrated less on listening and more on making sure your own
side was heard. When that happens, you are listening to your
partner with only half an ear, because you are busy formulating
your response. With the Imago process, the sender has a unique
opportunity to be truly heard, while the receiver can let go of the
need to respond right away. This frees the receiver from focusing on
his own version of the story, and he can focus instead on fully listening to the sender.

After the sender has shared, the receiver will then use mirroring, validation, and empathy (as described previously) to respond to the sender's statements. This will provide an opportunity to delve more deeply in a supportive way, without arguing or escalating defensiveness.

Throughout the book are Imago dialogue scripts for you and your partner to follow. Feel free to modify the questions if they don't seem relevant, or to add questions that you need answered.

Talking about the Affair

The first step in creating your new monogamy will be to commit yourself to fully understanding what happened and why your partner cheated. This process will mean having a series of conversations with each other. These conversations must be—first and foremost—honest, empathetic, and kind.

If you or your partner are still in the crisis phase of affair recovery and so overwhelmed by difficult emotions such as anger, defensiveness, guilt, or resentment that you can't communicate with openness and kindness using these tools, then you may choose to postpone these dialogues until you can find a little more distance from the pain of the affair. You may even choose to see a therapist or other counselor, either separately or together, to process some of the most painful feelings.

In fact, it may be easier to work with a therapist as you have these conversations. The most important thing to remember is that you both need to be willing to hear difficult truths about yourself and your relationship, and you must be willing to let go, at least for the length of the conversation, of damaging emotional expressions or behaviors that don't encourage truthful communication.

Damaging emotional expressions include name-calling and what I call "garbage-canning." Name-calling is anything that includes a derogatory and personalized insult to your partner. It also can include statements that begin with *globalizing*, which is saying things that start with "You always" or "You never." No one "always" or "never" does anything, so keep your conversation clear of globalized blame, accusations, and name-calling in order to have a clear discussion of your feelings.

Garbage-canning is when you bring every issue from the past into the same sentence or on top of one issue. If you are talking about a particular problem or frustration, try not to bring in all the other frustrations that you have had throughout your relationship. Try to use this issue as a way to practice communicating your needs. See if the two of you can mirror, validate, and empathize. Chances are that practicing these dialogue skills can help you with this particular frustration, and all the other problems from the past will either work out, or you can process them at another time. Don't try to throw everything in the can at once in an attempt to resolve it all. It can make your partner feel overwhelmed, and it won't resolve any of the conflict that you are struggling with in the moment.

Three Key Areas to Discuss

It's important to discuss what was happening in three key areas of your relationship prior to the affair. First, how did you stop communicating and in what areas? Second, did you feel appreciated, or in what ways did you stop appreciating each other or take each other for granted? And finally, what was happening in your sexual relationship?

For some couples, communication is the broad sky under which all else grows and flourishes. If your communication is positive, your relationship can withstand many things. But what does positive communication mean? For some it can be a fifteen-minute check-in every night. Maybe when you look back, you see that you and your partner have gone weeks without actually talking. Maybe you talked about what you would have for dinner, but did you really talk about your relationship, your future, or the things that mattered?

Expressing appreciation can also be at the bottom of the list of priorities when daily life seems like one long to-do list. When that list grows unmanageable and your partner doesn't seem to be helping lighten the load, resentment can build. Whereas it used to be a daily expression of delight, appreciation may now be merely a bone tossed for good behavior when one of you completes a chore around the house. If you don't feel appreciated or, worse, if you feel criticized, you may be vulnerable to anyone outside of your relationship who makes you feel special or valued. It can be very tempting to move toward someone who flatters you when you feel that your partner only points out what you do wrong.

What was going on in the bedroom prior to the affair? Although a lackluster sex life in no way justifies infidelity, exploring what was present in your erotic life prior to the affair can neutralize blame, not create more. If both of you felt trapped in a boring or routine sex life, it was the responsibility of both of you to change it. The one who cheats can't blame her partner for lack of passion. This is an excuse and a way to avoid taking responsibility. What was really happening in your love life? We will talk more about this in chapter 6.

The next series of exercises will give you a chance to begin discussing some of your feelings that you may have been stuck in, literally, from when the affair began. When you are ready to sit and talk, make an appointment with your partner for a dialogue. Ask your partner, "Is this a good time for a dialogue about the affair?" And if it isn't convenient for your partner, ask her to plan a time that works. It's important that the two of you have this time together, where you don't feel forced or rushed. Of course, one or both of you may not be thrilled about sitting down to talk about these difficult feelings, but it's important to agree on a mutual time and stick to it.

To prepare for your first conversation about the affair, set aside some time when you won't be disturbed for at least one hour. Turn off any distractions, such as cell phones, computers, or the television, and simply set aside this time to focus on one another.

Using a journal, take a few moments to write out the answers to the following sentence stems. When you are finished, sit with your partner and share your answers. Use the dialogue process (as outlined previously) to take turns being the sender and the receiver. The sender will have a chance to get out everything she needs to say, and the receiver will use mirroring to show the sender that she is being heard and seen. Then you will switch.

Exercise 2.1   The Dialogue Process

Sit where you will both be comfortable, and have a pad of paper and some pens handy. Remember that this conversation might be very difficult, but it's necessary for you to move through and heal from this wrenching time in both of your lives. I'll lead you through several conversations that will help you get to the root of the affair. Practice referring to the affair as "our" affair, since it happened to both of you. If you can get away from considering it as just your partner's affair, it will strengthen the bond between you, rather than allow it to distance you from one another.

Use the dialogue process to talk about the three areas: communication, appreciation, and your sex life, and how you each felt about these areas in your relationship prior to the affair. Share what it was like for you and what you weren't talking about then. You may find that, looking back, there were things on your mind that you couldn't express. Now that you consider how you felt before the affair began, you may have some new insight and understanding of your own behavior.

The receiver should mirror the sender after each sentence stem. Then wait until the sender has completed all of the sentence stems before using validation and empathy. This lets the sender get out all of his thoughts without interrupting their flow. If it helps, the receiver can write down the sender's answers to refer back to.

Remember, validation and empathy mean going over to your partner's side of the bridge to understand his perspective, not to agree, argue, or apologize. Simply acknowledging your partner's experience can be a powerful form of healing for both of you. When the conversation seems to be finished, switch roles and have the receiver be the sender.

You may want to do this exercise in two sittings, where you take a short break before switching roles.

Sender. One thing I have felt about our communication
is _____.

Receiver. [Mirror.]

Sender. One way I have contributed to our lack of communication
is _____.

Receiver. [Mirror.]

Sender. One thing I longed for in our communication before the affair was _____.

Receiver. [Mirror.]

Sender. I wish you could have appreciated me before the affair began by _____.

Receiver. [Mirror.]

Sender. I wish I could have appreciated you before the affair began by _____.

Receiver. [Mirror.]

Sender. One way I prevented us from appreciating each other was _____.

Receiver.   [Mirror.]

Sender.   What I longed for in our sex life before the affair was _____ .

Receiver.   [Mirror.]

Sender.   What I really wanted more of in our sex life before the affair was _____ .

Receiver.   [Mirror.]

Sender.   What I didn't know how to ask for in our sex life before the affair was _____ .

Receiver.   [Mirror.]

Sender.   One way I kept us stuck in our sex life was _____ .

Receiver.   [Mirror.]

Sender.   One thing I appreciate about you now is _____ .

Receiver.   [Mirror.]

Validate

Receiver.   Knowing you the way I do, some of the things you said made sense to me, like _____ . They made sense to me because _____ .

  or:

        Tell me more about _____ .

  Repeat validation.

Empathize

Receiver.   I imagine that you feel _____ . [Check out some feeling words with your partner; did your partner

feel those things?
Are there other things that your partner feels?]

Sender.   Sharing this with you, I feel _____ .

Receiver, mirroring. Thank you for sharing this with me.

Now switch roles and go back through the validation and empathy dialogues.

Appreciate

It's important that each of you send at least one appreciation for this dialogue when you are done.

Sender.   One thing I appreciated about this dialogue with you was _____ .

Receiver.   [Mirror.]

Now switch roles and go back through the appreciation dialogue.

After both of you have shared, mirrored, validated, and empathized, you should have some valuable (and possibly painful) information about how each of you felt prior to the affair.

If communication was an issue, you are already improving your communication skills simply by practicing this dialogue. By following these steps of mirroring, validating, and empathizing, you have powerfully shifted your relationship dynamic.

Continuing the Conversation

In the next series of conversations, you may want to agree to talk for a set amount of time (give yourselves thirty to sixty minutes), and then check in about whether you want to keep going or schedule a time to continue the talk later. These dialogues can be emotionally overwhelming, so you want to make sure that neither of you becomes too drained by them. You run the risk of derailing the dialogue back into conflict if you get too wiped out from the emotional struggle. However, don't avoid them just because they are hard. Try not to let more than a couple of days go by before you continue the conversation.

Exercise 2.2   Dialogue about the Turning Point in Your Relationship

You will begin this series of conversations by examining the turning point in your relationship: the beginning of your affair. Go back to when the affair began, and picture what was happening in your lives at the time. If you aren't sure when your partner started cheating, go back to a time when you suspect that the affair began.

What did you both feel at the time? To begin, get grounded by closing your eyes and getting comfortable in your chair. Imagine dropping out of your head and your thoughts, and going into your body and your feelings. When you think about the period when you believe the infidelity began, what emotion do you experience? Find this feeling in your body. Identify the shape, the heaviness, the sharpness of the emotion, and where you hold it in your body. Is it a color? Is it dark or light? See how much you can find in that feeling, and then share with your partner what that was like for you.

When I think about the beginning of the affair...

Sender.   In my body, I feel _____.

Receiver, *mirroring.* In your body, you feel _____.

Sender.   It feels like _____.

Receiver, *mirroring.* It feels like _____ .

Sender. I think the color and shape might be _____ .

Receiver, *mirroring.* You think the color and shape might
be _____ .

Sender. It is located _____ .

Receiver, *mirroring.* You feel it is located _____ .

Sender. I think it means that _____ .

Receiver, *mirroring.* You think it means that _____ .
[Offer validation and empathy.]

In this exercise, validation and empathy may be hard to express
when you are reflecting on your partner's experience of being in the
body. Concentrate on your partner's interpretation of the feelings in
the body. When your partner has shared what it means to her, can you
validate that? Validation in this instance might sound like "That makes
sense that it could mean this to you, because..."

Empathy in this instance might be simply trying to understand
your partner's emotions. "It sounds as if you may be feeling..." And
then make a guess about what those emotions might be. Check it out
with your partner. Is it correct? Are there other things your partner
might be feeling as well?

Now switch roles and repeat the dialogue portion of the exercise.
When you switch and your partner drops into his feelings, he may
have totally different and opposite emotions to share. Or he may have
felt the same emotion but experienced it in a different way in his body.

Share what you appreciate about this dialogue after you are done,
and mirror this for each other.

What didn't you talk about? Think back and try to identify what the
two of you may have been avoiding talking about or dealing with just
prior to the affair. Perhaps you weren't talking about the lack of

emotional connection with one another or that your sex life was becoming slightly boring. Or maybe you were completely avoiding talking about your developing feelings for someone outside of the relationship.

Notice whether the feelings that you are each sharing now are emotions that were kept secret at the time of the affair or even earlier. Ask yourselves these questions:

What feelings were you having at the time of the affair about your marriage that you avoided sharing with your partner?

Did you feel seen by your partner prior to the affair?

Did you feel that your partner listened to you?

Were you a good partner in your marriage? Why or why not?

Did you feel emotionally disconnected from your partner?

Did you feel that your sex life was less than satisfying?

Were you having feelings for someone else that you never talked about?

Were there things you wanted more of in your relationship that you didn't express?

Were you angry or resentful and couldn't tell your partner?

Did you feel lonely in your relationship?

What do you really want to know? Some experts say that the more you talk about the affair, the better. Sometimes, however, sharing too many details can reinjure the person who feels betrayed. Hearing about how beautiful the affair partner was or how great a lover he was can be hurtful. Comparing you to an outside partner may feel hostile. It can be a way to show anger and hurt instead of truly being transparent. Be sure you really want to know the details of the affair before you ask for them. Can you live with the answers to your questions? Ask yourself honestly, *What do I really want to know?*

The questions you ask regarding how many times they made love, where they met for lunch, or the size of the lover's body parts may not really give you the answers you need. Before having this discussion, consider carefully what details you want to know and why. If you want to force your partner to divulge details just to make him feel worse, reconsider this. Your affair-recovery time is meant to be a time of connection, not disconnection.

But if you want to know certain details for other reasons, then be honest with yourself and with your partner. Some examples of "need to know" details are questions about birth control or condoms. If you want to be sure that your partner wasn't exposed to a sexually transmitted disease, you may want to ask if protection was used. Or you may want to know the depth of your partner's emotional attachment to the other person. In that case, it would make sense to ask questions about your partner's feelings for the affair partner. Be clear about the real information you're after, and formulate your questions to get directly to those points.

It may not be the details of the cheating that you are curious about as much as the motivation for the affair. What did your partner really want during the infidelity? What kind of person did your partner become when he was with this other person? What was your partner afraid of during that time? Did your partner have fears at all? What were they? What did your partner like about himself during the affair? What didn't he like about himself? Did your partner think of you while he was with the other person?

Curiosity about all of these things and more is normal. And wondering why your partner was with that other person is also normal. Asking the right questions to learn about the parts of your partner that you don't know is vital. If you ask a question and your partner can't answer it, try asking it in a different way. Your partner may not be purposely withholding information from you, but may be unsure how to get to the answers.

What helps is to share with your partner what you hope to get from the discussion; for instance, "I hope that you will tell me what it felt like to come home every night, knowing that you were hiding this from me" instead of "Where did you go?" This may give you a clearer picture of what it was like for your partner as well.

You may want to use the following questions as a way to start the conversation. Some of these questions are about the outside relationship, some are about the dishonesty, and some are about the sexual relationship. Some of them are very typical questions that you may have gone over before. Make sure, this time, that you really want the answers, and don't ask the questions if you don't really want the truth.

"How did you meet?"

"How often did you meet?"

"Did you have sexual intercourse?"

"Did you fall in love?"

"Did you meet at work?"

"Did you meet the affair partner in our home?"

"Did you consider this person your best friend?"

"Did you pay this person for sex?"

"Did you cheat with this person because you were lonely?"

"Did you cheat with this person because you were mad at me?"

"Did you feel guilty?"

"Did you wonder what I would do if I found out?"

"Did you worry that I might discover the affair?"

"What did you do to hide it from me?"

"Did you consider a permanent future with this person?"

"Did this person care about you more than you cared about him?"

"Is this person married?"

"Does this person know about us?"

"Does this person's partner know the truth now?"

"How did you feel when you were with that person?"

"What were you afraid of during the affair?"

"What did you like about yourself during your affair?"

"What did you not like about yourself during that time?"

"What do you like about who you are now?"

"Did you think of me after you were with this person?"

"Did you ever wonder if I was cheating?"

"Did you think I would leave you if I found out?"

"Did you hope I would find out?"

"What was it like to come home to me after you were with this person?"

What did the affair mean? One way to address your questions is to move beyond asking for details, and ask yourself and your partner the following three simple questions:

"What did the affair mean about you?"

"What did the affair mean about us?"

"What did the affair mean about me?"

Each of you should ask yourselves these questions and then share your answers. See if you can find a place of empathy and understanding, even if the answers are painful or you don't approve of their origins.

When you consider what the affair meant about you, you may make up some stories right away about how you caused the affair or that your partner didn't love you enough to stay faithful. If your self-esteem is not strong right now, you might think that perhaps the affair meant you weren't attractive or sexy enough for your partner. Perhaps you didn't please your partner or provide enough erotic adventures. Maybe you weren't a good-enough provider. Or maybe you pushed your partner into someone else's arms. These are all stories that people commonly tell themselves about what an affair means about them. Challenge these beliefs that you hold about the affair. It may not really mean any of these things. These ideas may be someone else's story. Maybe you got these ideas from your parents, books you've read, or your friends. They may not have any truth to them, and you may just be using them as a way to beat yourself up. Or you may be using these stories as a way to feel sorry for yourself. If you are truly wondering what the affair can teach you about the ways in which you need to grow, then challenging your thoughts and what you believe about the affair can be valuable. Otherwise, negative thoughts are probably just a waste of energy.

When you think about what the affair meant about you as a couple, you may come to some conclusions about how your relationship was faring prior to the affair. We will delve more deeply into those thoughts next, when we talk about what you were both feeling when the affair began.

When you begin to question what the affair meant about your partner, you will have to start considering what kind of changes your partner may have been going through that made her cheat. Think back about what your partner was going through at the time. Do you remember how your partner felt about herself when the affair began? These are important questions and things you may want to discuss at length as you move into deeper conversations together.

Scheduling Check-Ins

Bring what you've learned from these exercises into your daily life by doing a daily check-in with your partner. Ask each other three things every day:

"How are you?"

"How am I?"

"How are we?"

Mirror each other, validate, and empathize if you can. This communication strategy will change the way you relate to each other. It can take fifteen minutes a day and shouldn't be an invitation to argue or rehash the affair every evening. If this happens, back off and skip to doing appreciations every evening instead, described next.

Daily Appreciations

You may have noticed that not feeling appreciated was a big issue for both of you before or during the affair. This is common and particularly bothersome to many couples. Our culture encourages boys from a young age to focus on their actions, what they *do*. When we meet a man for the first time, one of the first things we say is "Hello, nice to meet you; what do you *do*?" which sounds as if we are more interested in a man's accomplishments than who he is.

Raised to focus on how they do in sports, business, career, and finance, men take very personally their partners' criticism that they aren't doing something well or right. Appreciation means being recognized for being successful not only in their lives but also in their roles in the world.

For women, being appreciated is a recognition, and a reminder that they are seen. You don't have to tell them you love them every day, but why wouldn't you want to? You can never tell a woman that she is beautiful often enough, not because she forgets from day to day, obviously, or because she is shallow and needs compliments to feel whole. You tell her because feeling appreciated and loved helps her feel connected, just as it does for men. No one likes to feel criticized; that's clear. And everyone not only likes but also needs to feel wanted and loved. Appreciation is a way to show our partners that we notice them and that they are important in the world.

You don't have to wait until you are in conflict to do daily appreciations. Doing appreciations every day can only help your relationship. Offering three appreciations every day will change your relationship drastically and make your interactions more positive. Saying to one another "One thing I appreciate about you is…" sounds simple, but it can dramatically alter the pattern of negative communication in which you may find yourselves.

Offer appreciations every day. Tell your partner the things you appreciate about him, and focus your comments in a way that shows that you notice. Some examples are "I really appreciate the way you hold the door open for me" and "I really appreciate how thoughtful you were to bring me my coffee this morning." Appreciations can be simple or broader: "I really appreciate what a good father you are to our children" or "I appreciate how hardworking you are" is more global. Showing that you see what your partner does, that you notice that they are trying, can shift your relationship and set the stage for a hopeful future.

Monogamy, remember, is a practice. What is it that you need to practice in your relationship to have what you desire? As you move through the rest of the book, you'll explore this question in depth and learn, from your partner and yourself, how you can cocreate a more loving, connected, adventurous, and fulfilling relationship for both of you.

CHAPTER 3

Building Trust

When you think about moving forward into a new marriage, characterized by your new monogamy agreement, you may think, *My partner cheated on me; how can I trust that she will abide by the agreement we make now, when she couldn't live by the one we made when we first committed to one another?* This is a valid question, and one you will probably continue to struggle with. This is the number one reason to keep talking to your partner and renegotiating your agreement.

Melanie and Todd had been married for several years when Todd found out she had been cheating. They talked it out, finally went to therapy, and were committed to staying together, but Todd was nervous. Melanie had hooked up with her ex-boyfriend several times a year since she and Todd had been married. She traveled often for business to the city where the ex-boyfriend lived. After the affair, her work schedule required her to travel the same amount and to the same places, but she insisted that she was no longer connected to her ex.

Todd was worried that Melanie was still communicating with her ex. Todd asked her for her e-mail and social network passwords for proof that she wasn't lying to him. Because she felt devastated that she had caused her husband so much pain, she gave him her passwords. Todd found himself obsessively checking her accounts several times a day, to the point where he couldn't focus on work or his other interests. When he wasn't checking her accounts, he was thinking about checking them.

Eventually, he realized that his obsession with and distrust of Melanie was hurting their relationship and killing him. He wasn't sleeping, he stopped eating regularly, his work productivity dropped off, and even though he and Melanie had decided to stay together and work it out, they were barely speaking. Melanie knew he was checking up on her, which made her feel worse than she already felt, causing her, in turn, not to trust *him*. And Todd simply couldn't seem to get over the fact that she had lied to him for so many years, pretending that nothing was going on. He didn't know how he could trust her again. He wasn't sure whether his fears were reasonable.

If you sense that your partner is going outside your agreement, you have to talk about these feelings right away. Your suspicions may or may not be right. Talk to your partner and use empathy, validation, and the other communication tools that you are learning in this book. Don't avoid the conversation because you aren't sure. Confront your fears.

When Todd finally sat Melanie down and said, "Look, I'm losing it here. I don't know if it's me and I just can't get past my fears because of what happened, or if something is still going on. But I can't settle down my paranoia. I need to know if there's anything I need to worry about or if it's just my fear talking."

Melanie was honest with Todd at that point: "Todd, your intuition is telling you something is off because it's true; my ex-boyfriend is still pursuing me. He calls me weekly and is trying to get me to see him. I never wanted to tell you, because I don't respond to him; I don't call him back. But I felt that if I told you, it would make things worse. Nothing is happening, but maybe your intuition is telling you something—like trust your gut; something is off—and then your mind is taking off on that."

Todd felt better because he knew that Melanie was telling him the truth, even though she worried that it would be the last straw for him, knowing that there was contact between her and her ex. Yet if he hadn't brought it up, he would have continued to feel like a detective and made himself sick, worrying and wondering if he was crazy.

But Todd can never really be sure that Melanie is telling him the whole truth. Maybe she will only tell him partial truths for the rest of their lives together. Maybe she is still lying. How can he know? Trust means learning to heed your own inner voice that tells you to relax and know that you will be all right, no matter what.

How Can You Trust Again?

Most people who have experienced infidelity in their relationships talk extensively and constantly about the need for trust. Betrayed partners want to learn to trust that their partners won't stray again. They want to trust that what their partners tell them is the truth. If their partner says the outside lover is out of the picture, they want to believe this. They want to trust their partners when they say they will change. And they really want to learn to trust their own instincts again; how could they have let themselves down this way? Their own intuition should have told them that something was wrong—and they should have listened to it.

The partners who had an affair want to learn to trust as well. They want to trust that if they stay in the marriage, things will be better and they will have a chance at happiness. They want to trust that they are making the right decision in letting go of the affair. They want to trust that their partners will stop distrusting them (will stop searching through their e-mail and phone records, for example). They want to know that their partners believe they have ended the affair. And they want to know that their partners believe in them and in their word.

Remember that trust is breached when there has been any type of violation of the implicit and explicit expectations in the relationship. An explicit agreement is one that you've stated to your partner, and it's obvious when it is broken. If you explicitly stated that you and your partner would not sleep with other people and your partner had a sexual affair, your partner broke your agreement.

An implicit assumption is something that you may have assumed your partner agreed to, but never explicitly stated. It may seem obvious—*if we're married, we won't have sex with anyone else*—but if this was never stated, then you can't actually accuse your partner of breaking your agreement, even though it may feel as if trust has been breached. This seems, to most of us, to be a fundamental understanding of a monogamy agreement, but what about subtler interpretations?

Jack went to a bachelor party with his friends the night before his colleague's wedding. The guys there did the usual bachelor-party stuff, according to Jack. They drank and employed a stripper, who performed oral sex on several of the guys. Jack went home that night, and when his wife, Elaine, asked him about the party, he casually joked about the sex in the back room. Elaine was horrified. She couldn't believe that the men Jack hung out with would operate this way, allowing a woman to perform fellatio on them in a public place for money in front of other guys. And worse yet, each of these men was married, and one's wife was a friend of Elaine. Jack hung his head and sheepishly admitted that he had participated as well. She was mortified. "I didn't think it was such a big deal," Jack said. "This is what guys do. I can't believe you didn't know." Elaine said, "I knew; I just didn't think you would do this to me after we got married."

One of the crucial concepts of the new monogamy is making implicit agreements explicit, so that both partners know exactly what the agreements are in the relationship. Some implicit assumptions are not as obvious as "Don't cheat." Sometimes they are more subtle expectations like "Don't show someone else attention." Your partner may not know that this is important to you. And your partner may not agree that this limitation is acceptable in your relationship. But if you don't talk about it, you never have the chance to find out.

How do you develop trust again? Feeling comfortable that you each know the implicit and explicit expectations, and that you both agree to and want to live by them will increase your trust in one another.

It may not happen right away. Trust, like forgiveness, will happen when you're ready. Read through this chapter to develop some skills and insight that will help you begin to regain trust in your own intuition. Your partner will need to work diligently to help you rebuild your trust in him, and will need to be scrupulously honest for the time being. Reading this chapter will help you develop trust in a general sense.

Trust Is Not about Apologizing

Trust is not about how many times someone says "I'm sorry." If that were the case, then apologies would automatically restore trust and couples would move on from breaches of trust without issue (or the need for this book). This doesn't mean that you should never apologize or forgive. Apologies offered in the spirit of true remorse and forgiveness, and given in generosity can be very healing. But they are not enough.

Forgiveness is granted over time, and is not bestowed with just those three words "I forgive you." Forgiveness is a living attitude that grows organically with time and the development of empathy. It cannot be forced.

Sometimes "I'm sorry" is simply a way of asking to be let off the hook. It can be a way of responding to accusations while avoiding telling the whole truth. Saying "I'm sorry" can be a way of asking the betrayed partner to let go of anger. An "I'm sorry" comes with the expectation that forgiveness should come after the apology, especially if it is heartfelt. This implies that there is something owed by the betrayed partner for the apology.

But just because someone apologizes doesn't mean that the apology is hitting home, relieving the pain, or making anything better. And it doesn't guarantee that the cheating partner won't cheat again.

Furthermore, it doesn't guarantee that the accuser will be distracted from anger. And forgiveness, if it is genuine, is not an automatic response. Forgiveness is not something that is given freely in response to an apology, although it may be said casually to appease the one who is apologizing. Forgiveness happens when the betrayed partner feels empathy for the partner who had the affair.

Finding out your partner cheated is an existential blow to the ego. It's like finding out that you are suddenly thrown from your throne, the highest seat in the kingdom, the seat that made you feel as if you were the most important person in the world. Discovering that you were actually replaceable to the one person who was supposed to regard you as the most uniquely important person can feel—emotionally, physically, sexually, and spiritually—as if you have lost your place in the universe. An "I'm sorry" rarely makes up for that crisis of self-worth.

If your partner seems genuinely remorseful but you still find that you can't forgive, don't worry. Let yourself heal on your own time. If forgiveness happens, it will do so as you and your partner are able to slowly feel empathy, and regain intimacy and eventually trust.

The Importance of Empathy and Validation

Without *empathy*—the ability to understand another's emotional experience—there can be no healing. Empathy is the true path to understanding after an affair, and is also a vital tool on the road to your new monogamy. With empathy you can each share your experiences and fears, and trust that your partner will make a real effort to understand what your feelings mean to you.

You don't have to agree with each other, apologize, or even try to change for the other person, but finding empathy for one another means that you make an effort to hear each other's hopes and fears, and put yourself in the other person's shoes. This may mean really feeling what it must have been like to experience the affair—from both sides.

If you don't believe that your partner will understand your feelings, it can be hard to disclose much of anything. However, if you are at an impasse and not making any progress in your conversations, it may not be your partner's fault. If you feel that your partner isn't answering your questions or moving into a more honest and open dialogue, you may want to ask yourself if you are truly being an empathetic listener.

People won't take the risk of sharing their vulnerability if they can't trust that their feelings will be heard. Telling someone "You shouldn't feel that way" or "When are you going to stop feeling that?" sends the message that the person's feeling experience is wrong. This causes the person to shut down, or get defensive or angry. Your partner simply wants to be heard and understood, just as you do.

As discussed in the previous chapter, validation and empathy may include phrases like "It makes sense to me that you might feel that way" or "Knowing you and what you have been through, I can understand that you would feel this way." If you are having trouble trusting that your partner is open to your experience, look at your own communication style and make sure you're expressing validation and empathy when you speak. Open communication works both ways.

When there is validation, relationship conflicts become less about who is the victim and who is the betrayer. Couples who are comfortable with empathy recognize their own potential to hurt each other, and thus often feel less blame when confronting traumatic experiences in the relationship.

Exercise 3.1   Trust and Empathy Dialogue

It can be hard to start the conversation about what it will take to build trust between you. You and your partner may fear one another's contempt, criticism, judgment, or misunderstanding. But if you are to heal from the affair and build a new monogamy, you must make an effort to first understand one another's experience.

This exercise will help you talk about your experience with the infidelity and begin to regain trust in each other. Remember that, as I explained in the previous chapter, with this dialogue technique, one person is the sender and the other the receiver, and the receiver will use validation and empathy as tools to help the sender feel heard and understood. At the end of this dialogue, you'll switch roles—the sender will become the receiver and vice versa—and repeat.

How the affair was for me:

Sender.   One of the ways I felt about myself during the affair, was _____ .

Receiver.   [Mirror.]

Sender.   One thing I've learned about myself since then
is _____ .

Receiver.   [Mirror.]

Sender.   One way I protected myself with the affair
was _____ .

Receiver.   [Mirror.]

Now switch roles.

Sender.   One of the ways that I punished you during that time
was _____ .

Receiver.   [Mirror.]

Now switch roles.

Sender.   One of the ways I used the affair was _____ .

Receiver.   [Mirror.]

Now switch roles.

Sender.   One way I am afraid I have lost myself now
is _____ .

Receiver.   [Mirror.]

Now switch roles.

Sender.   One thing I can't give up that I've found in me
is _____ .

Receiver.   [Mirror.]

Now switch roles.

Sender.   One way that I have grown from all of this
is _____ .

Receiver.   [Mirror.]

Now switch roles.

Validate

Receiver.   Knowing you the way I do, that makes sense to me
because _____ .

or:

Tell me more about _____ .

Empathize

Receiver.   I imagine that you feel _____ .

Sender.   Sharing this with you, I feel _____ .

Receiver, mirroring. Thank you for sharing this with me.

It's important to validate and empathize at the end of mirroring. These parts of the process are what make your partner feel not only seen and heard, but also understood. It's like telling your partner that she's not crazy for feeling as she does. It doesn't mean you feel the same, but using validation and empathy means that you are striving to really make sense of what your partner is going through.

You don't have to agree with what your partner says, say "I'm sorry," or ask for forgiveness, although you may be drawn to do so. Letting your partner know that you get what she says can often be enough.

Learning to Trust Your Own Instincts

Trust is not about wishing and hoping that your partner will change, or hoping that he will behave in a certain way. Wishing and hoping your partner will change won't move you forward in your healing. Trust is about learning to rebuild and establish trust in your own self. You can't make your partner responsible for your ability to trust in the world. Regardless of what happens with your relationship, you will always need to be able to trust yourself, your inner voice, and your own intuition about the world, with or without your partner.

Learning to trust your own instincts again is even more important than trying to learn to trust someone who has cheated. The goal after an affair is to rebuild trust in your own intuition. This is where you have been the most thrown off balance: in your own inner knowing. You may be wondering what happened to that inner voice you had always relied on to tell you the truth. Your intuition may have told you that your partner was cheating, but you didn't listen. Or maybe you knew, somewhere deep inside, that something was wrong, and you purposely ignored it.

Many women who come to my office say they had known something was wrong, that they had "felt" as if something were off and suspected their spouses of cheating, but that they "didn't want to know" so they turned off that inner voice that had warned them to watch for the signs.

Or maybe you didn't sense that anything was wrong, and now have no idea how to begin to trust yourself when your partner tells you he won't cheat again. How do you trust your intuition when it let you down?

Later in this chapter is an exercise designed to help you get in touch with that inner voice, that quiet place inside that will help you differentiate between fear and intuition. Finding that inner voice again and learning to trust your gut will help you rely on your own inner knowing. In this way, you will always know the truth. When someone tells you something, you will just "know" whether he is being real or something is off about what he is saying. You will be able to go inside and use your inner barometer to judge the situation.

Inner-Truth Monitor

Your inner-truth monitor is a barometer that helps you distinguish what's real from what's a lie. The problem is that many half-truths contain just enough truth to be convincing, especially if we really want to believe them. We choose to turn off the rest of what we intuitively "know" is true in order to live with only the truth that we can handle.

In hindsight, we always understand more now than we did then. Looking back, you may realize that there were signs that something was wrong that you chose to ignore. Ask yourself the following questions and see if you knew more than you were willing to admit, or if there were signs along the way that you missed. It's irrelevant now whether or not you knew or ignored all the signs. What's important now is to learn to trust your own instincts going forward so that when someone tells you something, you can tune in to your inner-truth monitor to see what rings true and what feels like deception.

Exercise 3.2 Develop Your Inner-Truth Monitor

Ask yourself the following questions, record your answers, read the intuition response, and write your feelings and responses:

1. Did you know your partner was cheating during the affair?
    Intuition response: Whether you answered yes or no, your intuition helped you deal with only as much as you could handle at the time. How clever of you to use your intuition to determine what you were ready to absorb. This means that you have an

intuitive sense that can be more highly developed over time. Give yourself quiet time every day to listen to your breathing. Trust that your inner "knowing" is guiding you toward the truth every day. Trust what you know.

2. Did you find signs of the affair at the time?

   Intuition response: Whether you answered yes or no, your intuition protected you from knowing the whole truth. Our inner selves will only give us so much information, only enough for us to handle. Our senses will screen out any information that will over-load us. Good for you that you only took in as many clues as your senses could process at one time. This means that you are a highly sensitive person. This sensitivity may mean that you feel things in a greater way than others do. This can be both joyful and overwhelming at times. Take time every day to move and stretch. Breathe deeply and with awareness. Surround yourself with beau-tiful scents and sights. Trust what you see and feel.

3. Did you suspect something was going on and try to confront your partner?

   Intuition response: Whether you answered yes or no, your inner gut, your center, was working toward your highest good by taking care of you. It helped you confront your partner in the best way you knew how at the time. Today you are learning even more skills to talk about difficult topics in your relationship. You can give yourself credit that you followed that inner voice and attempted to deal with the affair in a direct way. This means that you are very sensitive to an inner voice that tells you right from wrong and your own inner truth. Take time every day to listen to silence and to sur-round yourself with beautiful sound. Focus on your inner voice, and know that you are always given the right answers. Trust what you hear.

Why Didn't You Trust Your Gut?

You may have had an inkling that something was wrong. Maybe things felt a little off in your relationship, but you ignored the warning signs. Maybe you wanted to give your partner the benefit of the doubt, or maybe you didn't want to believe it was true that your partner could be cheating. Perhaps you wanted to think of yourself as a progressive person who could handle whatever your monogamy was becoming. So maybe you buried your gut instincts and the small voice inside that told you the truth: that your partner was being unfaithful.

Even when we say "I had no idea," we may look back and realize there were signs along the way. Not trusting that you knew the truth may lead you to feel negatively about yourself, and can lead to some depressed feelings. Go easy on yourself and give your gut a break.

Protecting yourself from hurt is a natural process. Now is the time to regain control over your own feelings by beginning to forgive yourself. Whether you had an inner knowing, a thought, or even a fear, let all of that be okay by first forgiving yourself.

Exercise 3.3   Forgive Yourself

Take this moment to breathe in deeply. Breathe out while saying to yourself *With every breath, I let go of judging myself.* Taking deep breaths, imagine letting all of that anger at yourself roll off your shoulders. If you feel sad or disappointed that you didn't listen to your inner knowing, tell yourself often *I am letting go of judgment,* and imagine all of that negative energy that is directed toward yourself washing down through your feet and flowing into the ground. Let the earth absorb what you can no longer hold in your body. You may find yourself standing stronger and taller, and feeling less drained of energy by the end of the day.

Let yourself be gentle when you realize that at times, in fact, your gut may have been wrong. Fear and intuition can sometimes feel the same. Sometimes you may have felt as if your gut were screaming at you *This is the truth!* only to find that it was your fear leading you down the wrong path. That may have led to some real confusion.

Tell yourself *I let go of all harsh judgment against myself,* and imagine a cool waterfall flowing over you and flowing down into the earth. Take some deep breaths. Now practice going to a powerful place inside. Go to your center. Take some more deep breaths. If you find yourself judging yourself again, repeat some of the previous statements. Imagine letting go of all of your harsh judgments against yourself and allowing them to flow down into the earth.

Regaining Control by Trusting Yourself Again

Early on, when we make a commitment to each other, we form a vision of the partnership and trust our own vision. We believe that our expectations are real and assume that our partners share that vision. Even if we never verbalize our assumptions and never make an explicit promise, after infidelity it can feel as if a promise has been broken, because we expected that our partners would be faithful to us.

Assuming that our partners would never sleep with someone else is a rational assumption in most cases, but when we learn that we assumed incorrectly, we are not only angry and hurt, but also disappointed in ourselves. We feel out of control, because we no longer have a grip on what we thought was rational. Learning to trust ourselves again means taking back control.

Listening to Your Inner Voice

To move into the new monogamy with a sense of trust, it's necessary to trust your own gut instinct: that inner knowing that you may have ignored during the affair. Learning to trust what is real can take time.

Remember, there's a difference between the fear that something bad is happening and intuition. In the early stages of affair recovery, you may confuse the two. You may feel anxious and fearful, certain that your partner is continuing to cheat, and believe that this is your deeper intuition talking, when it may only be fear based on your experience with the affair. At this stage, it's best not to make any major decisions or determine that you know what's going on in your partner's head or heart, because fear will have clouded your ability to listen to your intuition.

Learning to differentiate between your actual intuition and what fear is telling you takes practice. It means going inside and listening to that quiet place at your center. That quiet voice is your intuition, or your gut instinct (Cooper 2000).

You may experience intuition as an inner knowing that seems calmer than the voice that tells you to be afraid. Going inside to discern between your anxiety about the future and your intuition can be challenging, but to move forward (on your own or with your partner), you have to get in touch with the difference.

Learning to trust your instincts is important in order to believe that your partner is being honest. To feel safe, you have to learn to trust your own inner voice, have confidence in that quiet inner knowing. Trust is an inside job.

For many of us, unfortunately, trust comes after we learn what it feels like to be lied to. Only then does our intuition know what that feels like, so then we can also know what honesty feels like. Trust means not doubting yourself. People who trust themselves don't second-guess their first instincts. They jump the first time, without being reckless. They trust their inner adult. Consult yours right now.

Exercise 3.4   Your Inner Child, Your Inner Critic, and Your Inner Adult

One way to learn to listen to your instincts is to become familiar with your other inner voices.

Ask yourself three questions right in this moment:

- *What does my inner child want right in this moment?*

- *What does my inner critic want right in this moment?*

- *What does my inner adult want right in this moment?*

Notice the difference among your three responses. If you have three totally different answers, you are on the right track. Notice what your inner child wants. It may feel good in the moment but not be good for you in the long run. Or it's an emotional response to something that may not be in your best interest over time. Or your inner child may want comfort or love.

Notice now what your inner critic wants. It's probably something that will shut down your creativity and spontaneity, perhaps based on fear of failure. It may tell you you're not good enough.

Now notice what your inner adult wants. This is probably something that will lead you onto a path of balance and creativity. And it most likely is a voice you can trust.

Differentiate among these three voices when you aren't sure what to trust when you are trying to find answers. Dividing into these three parts of yourself can help you learn to trust the voice inside that is reliable, grown-up, and in your best interest.

Exercise 3.5 Feel the Power and Let Go of Control

Practice the following visualization:

Imagine for a moment that you are standing at the mouth of a river. Feel yourself standing in the river up to your knees. Notice which way the river is flowing. Is it moving away from you toward the ocean, or is it flowing toward you from the ocean? Just notice it.

Today is different from all other days. Notice if what you need today is water that comes from the powerful ocean, with its waves and mighty tides, water that flows into the river and fills you up.

Or it may be that today you feel the river flowing away from you, releasing its energy and joining as it flows away from you and empties into the open ocean, being absorbed into the mighty sea. As you imagine this river and yourself standing in it, you may actually feel the pull of the river toward the ocean, away from you.

You can feel the river pulling at your legs, as the sand at your feet shifts. The river might be rushing away, and you may feel its cool ripples against your skin. Or you may actually feel the rush as it runs toward your body, pushing against you, almost trying to knock you over.

Depending on the day, or even the moment in which you do this exercise, you may feel the river running in one direction or the other. And some days you may even feel the river at a totally still moment, where you stand. And yet the ocean is never still, and the river that runs to it or is filled by it is constant. You, too, are constantly affected by its power. And your intuition will tell you which you need at any given moment. Do you need to absorb the power or release it right in this moment?

If you can learn to trust yourself again, then you can begin to trust your inner power. When you can trust yourself, you will be able to listen to that inner voice that tells you what's right for you.

Jill and Jackson had been married for seven years. Jill admitted that she had been telling herself and everyone around her a "story" about Jackson's affair for a long time: "I told everyone that Jackson messed around on me and that I was so shocked when I found out. I told my family that when I married him, I had no clue that this would ever happen. All my friends were so surprised that he cheated. I always told everyone that he was such a stand-up guy and that this came out of nowhere.

"And yet, Jackson and I met when he was still married to someone else. How could I really believe that he would be faithful to me when he cheated on his last wife? I wanted to believe that I was special, different. But I knew on some level that things had changed between us after we'd married. When we got married, he started treating me the way he used to treat his ex-wife. I knew what was happening. I just didn't know how to stop it. I told everyone I had no idea what was going on, but I think I was just too scared to admit that I saw it coming. Now we are reevaluating our whole relationship.

"He realizes that he has been repeating a pattern, one that he has repeated his whole life probably. And now we are deciding whether we want to make this relationship work. But we have to have a new monogamy, a new type of marriage. We can't do it the way we have always done it in the past. Our marriage has to be an open-communication marriage, where we talk about our fears and feelings, and if we start to feel ourselves going down that old path, we need to talk. I don't even care if it brings us to some scary places. I just don't want to go into that denial place again.

"I have to learn to trust myself and know that I can confront the truth at any time. I have to know that I can confront him and that we won't return to those old patterns and avoid talking about what's happening. Jackson agrees. He's unhappier than I am, and he doesn't want to feel as if he is in denial either. We want to wake up and be real with each other."

Exercise 3.6   Meditation for Self-Trust

Finding calm inner knowing takes practice. One way to practice tuning in to your inner knowing is *mindfulness*, which simply means paying attention to what is here, in this moment.

If you are feeling fear right in this moment, then you are probably worrying about what hasn't happened yet. To get out of your fear, return to this present moment, focusing on finding your intuitive voice and what it's saying right now. Your intuition is in the now, in this present moment.

This is not an easy job. If it were, we wouldn't have to practice. Meditation is a practice. Meditation practitioners spend a lifetime learning to be in the moment to find quiet and listen to the inner voice.

This exercise will help you begin your practice of finding your intuition. Meditation is the act of becoming mindful, and this is a simple mindful-meditation practice. Try to find time every day to sit quietly. You may, at first, feel restless and uneasy, but as you make time in your schedule, you will find that the sitting and listening become easier, and that you look forward to this time in your busy life.

This practice is especially helpful if you are feeling fearful or anxious. Meditation will help you calm your fearful thoughts and hear your inner voice, allowing you to trust your own inner truth.

Exercise 3.7   Meditation for Finding Inner Truth

Take some time to sit quietly and listen to your inner voice. This exercise will help you still all the noise in your mind by letting your thoughts float through without your getting hooked by them.

1. Find a quiet place to sit or lie down. Breathe deeply, taking breaths in through your nose and releasing them through your mouth.

2. Breathe into your lower belly and feel the clean, new air coming in. Exhale the old, stale air out of your body.

3. Give yourself permission to enjoy this moment that you have to yourself. There's nowhere you need to go and nothing else you need to do in this moment.

4. Find a quiet place in your center and drop into that safe place. Try to envision a warm, beautiful center within, where you can rest. Now tell yourself that you are safe and can trust your intuition.

5. Notice the fears as they circle inside, even in your safe place. Let them just slide by. Notice but don't try to analyze, judge, or change them. Watch them slide by on an inner screen, the way clouds float by in the sky.

6. Your center may be in your solar plexus, about two inches above your navel, or you may feel it somewhere else. Take some deep breaths into that center and let them go.

7. If you have a question you would like to meditate on, think of it now and hold it lightly in mind. Try not to focus too intently on hearing the answer. Now notice what you feel in your center. What comes up for you? Breathe. Take some more deep breaths into your

center. Now go back to noticing your question. Find your center with your awareness, and breathe into that space now. What do you notice to be true in your center? You may hear or notice a word or phrase, or experience a knowing in your intuitive senses. Know that this may be fear or intuition. Just notice without judgment.

8. If it's fear, it will circle, making you feel anxious. If it's "knowing," it will bring calm. Either way, let it go without judgment. Imagine it as a cloud that floats gently across your inner consciousness. Watch it go by; don't hold on to it. Go back to your inner self. Breathe deeply. Drop into your calm center. Listen quietly. Breathe. Feel. Ask your question again if you want. Breathe. Notice whether you see a word or phrase in your mind or center. Or you may see a picture or symbol in your mind. Just notice and let it go. You may feel anxious or experience an inner "knowing" that this is your answer. You may not get anything, and that's okay too. Just breathe.

9. Breathe in and be grateful for the moment. Exhale fully and be grateful for this new moment. Thank your inner self for taking this time. Thank your higher self for trusting your intuition and knowing that whatever answer you receive is exactly what you need right now. Trust that whatever you receive will be clear to you now or later, perhaps in a dream. Give yourself a moment to appreciate that you took the time to listen to your true self.

10. Whenever you are ready, take a deep breath and come all the way back to your body and your surroundings. Take your time, stretching and taking some deep, cleansing breaths.

You may want to write down what you remember or go ahead and move into your day, enjoying your sense of inner knowing. You can come back to your safe inner place anytime.

Discussing Anxiety and Fear with Your Partner

The way to trust one another again, as well as to develop trust in yourself and your instincts, is to discuss openly what each of you is experiencing in the aftermath of the affair. You both are probably experiencing fear, anxiety, distrust, and perhaps even excitement and attraction, which may be hard to discuss together. The only way to work through the complexities of these experiences is to talk about them as honestly as possible.

Some ways to share your fears with your partner as you move into this new phase of your relationship is to use the dialogue skills you are gaining in this book. Anxiety is usually fear about the future or things that haven't happened yet. That doesn't mean that those fears aren't real for you or that they aren't painful to talk about, but usually, they haven't actually happened.

As we discussed in the previous chapter, using "I" statements will keep the focus on expressing your own emotions. This reduces the perception that you are trying to control your partner's behavior, because you are not blaming your feelings on your partner. If you think about the different feelings in these two statements, it makes sense that "I" statements are less inflammatory: "I am frightened" differs from "You are scaring me."

Have a dialogue in which your partner can mirror what you share so that you know that she hears you and understands your feelings. Your partner doesn't have to change or make things better; she only has to empathize to let you know that your fears are valid and that they make sense for you.

Exercise 3.8 Fear and Anxiety Dialogue

This dialogue exercise can help each of you when you are feeling some anxiety about the future or anything that's happening with your relationship. Remember to choose a time and place when and where you both feel safe and comfortable to share. And remember to mirror each other, and then validate and empathize.

Validation means telling your partner that it makes sense that he has those feelings. And empathy means trying to understand how your partner feels, even if you don't agree or you feel differently.

Sometimes I am afraid:

Sender.   What I want you to know is _____ .

Receiver.   [Mirror.]

Sender.   When I see you hurting, _____ .

Receiver.   [Mirror.]

Sender.   What scares me when I see you hurting
           is _____ .

Receiver.   [Mirror.]

Sender.   What I want for us is _____ .

Receiver, mirroring. It makes sense that you
           feel _____ [summarize sender's statements],
           because _____ .

Sender.   Yes, and _____ .

Receiver, mirroring. It makes sense that you feel that too,
           because _____ . And I imagine that you also
           feel _____ .

Sender. [Yes or no.] And I feel _____ .

Receiver. [Mirror.]

Sender. One thing I appreciate about this dialogue with you is _____ .

Receiver. One thing I appreciate about this dialogue with you is _____ .

Now switch roles and do the exercise again.

Barbara and Keith were very anxious about whether or not they could make their future work. Barbara had cheated on Keith early on in their relationship, and yet they had married and had children anyway, hoping things would settle into normal and they could work out whatever had caused the affair. With work, children, and moving from town to town due to Keith's military service, they never found the time or developed the communication skills to process what had happened. They moved beyond it, but Keith harbored deep resentment: "I never really trusted Barbara after that. I always checked her e-mail and her phone records. I had all her passwords, and from time to time, I was obsessed with thoughts that she would do it again. How could I let her do this to me? It was driving me crazy, and I wondered why I ever married her. But then I would look at our children and realize how much I really loved her. My gut told me she really loved me too, but I could never really be sure. My fear was constantly running me around."

I gave Barbara and Keith the meditation exercise to practice mindfulness and be in the moment. This was a new experience for Keith, who was always focused on the future or the past: "I always worried about what I had to do next or what had happened in the past in our relationship. I always felt anxious or depressed. Then I started this meditation practice. At first it was hard; all I could do was sit and breathe for about three or four minutes at a time. But eventually I started to feel a shift. I found that I could sit for longer periods of time and that my mind wandered less. And it started to help me in my work too. I actually had a clearer sense of what to do in my job."

Barbara noticed a difference too: "When Keith told me one day that he was no longer obsessing about the past, I wasn't sure I believed him. We did the dialogue 'What I want you to know is...,' and he told me that he wanted me to know that he wasn't afraid that I was still cheating; he was afraid that he could no longer trust his instincts. He was so scared about that, because he has to live in the world and do his work with his guys trusting him, and he needs to trust his own instincts to keep them alive most days. So when he told me that, it was the first time that he had discussed how scared he was, not how angry he was. It changed everything for us. I was able to share with him that what I wanted for us was to be able to discuss our fears, but not let them rule our relationship. I want Keith to trust me, but more important, I want him to trust himself."

Barbara and Keith practice by checking in with each other. They share their feelings and validate them, instead of accusing each other of being paranoid. They use empathy and respond when one of them talks about fears, by saying, "It makes sense that you feel that, because..." This helps both of them feel safer about discussing their fears, and helps them distinguish between fear and intuition. They each practice the meditation on their own, and talk about any anxiety that comes up about their future.

Exercise 3.9   Anxiety about the Future

Another dialogue that helps when you are feeling anxious about starting a new monogamy focuses on the future. Starting fresh in an old relationship and relearning to trust both yourself and your partner can be scary and exciting. Some days can feel easier than others. This dialogue is for those days when the future feels particularly scary.

Sender.   What scares me when I think about the future
is _____ .

Receiver.   [Mirror.]

Sender.   What I can't stop thinking about is _____ .

Receiver.   [Mirror.]

Sender.   What I need from you each day is _____ .

Receiver.   [Mirror.]

Sender.   What I need from you when I tell you my feelings
is _____ .

Receiver.   It makes sense that you feel _____ [summarize
sender's statements], because _____ .

Sender.   Yes, and _____ .

Receiver,   *mirroring.* It makes sense that you feel that too,
because _____ . And I imagine you also
feel _____ .

Sender.   [Yes or no.] And I feel _____ .

Receiver.   [Mirror.]

Sender.   One thing I appreciate about this dialogue with you
is _____ .

Receiver. One thing I appreciate about this dialogue with you
is _____ .

Now switch roles and repeat.

Trust Takes Patience

When you're learning to trust yourself and your partner all over again, you may feel moments of fear, anxiety, frustration, and even despair. You may feel that you can never trust your partner or that you can never believe your inner knowing again, since they both let you down. But trust is a process. With empathy, openness, self-awareness, and patience, you can build a solid, trusting love relationship again. When you feel as if it will never happen, use the tools in this chapter to connect once again with yourself and your partner.

The tools you have learned in this chapter include the importance of empathy; dialogue skills like mirroring, validating, and empathizing; talking about your fear; learning to trust your own instincts; trusting your gut; the difference between fear and intuition; meditation and mindfulness; sharing your anxiety about the future; and finding patience.

After a while, you will notice a new trust growing. It may not happen all at once, and you may always have areas of life where you have trouble trusting, but if you nurture trust, you will experience it building anew in yourself and your partner.

In the next chapter, you will begin to create a new vision of your life together, where you can start to explore options you may never have considered for your monogamy.

CHAPTER 4

Creating a Vision of Your New Relationship

"The affair was a whack on the side of the head," explained Ellen. "At first I thought, *It's his fault*, and then I thought, *Maybe not; it must have been my fault*. But after we discussed it at length, we realized that maybe it wasn't helpful to blame either of us totally for what happened. This was just so unlike both of us. Our lives had ended up so different from how we had planned. And neither of us wanted to end our marriage."

Ned was surprised that Ellen, his wife, would consider staying with him after his affair. He wanted to handle their relationship very differently this time. He wanted to talk about their monogamy and define it in ways that worked for both of them: "For me, monogamy always meant the man worked while the woman stayed home. Well, that didn't work for Ellen. So that was the first rewrite. And we never talked about it in the past. She was unhappy, and I was put off by her returning to work after the kids were born. Then she was unhappy when I wanted a life of my own, playing golf every weekend and going out with the boys. But that's what I thought marriage was. My dad did it, my brothers, my uncles, even my friends. It was what I assumed I was supposed to do. She didn't like it. I thought, *The hell with that; I'll find someone who understands me!* I should have understood what was going on with us. We were making all kinds of assumptions about what monogamy was supposed to look like."

"Ned didn't like it," Ellen said. "I would be on the phone all night when he got home from work. I had a male colleague, and Ned would get jealous and upset when he and I spoke on the phone after work. I look back now and realize that my monogamy expectation was different from his. Mine included male friends, and his didn't, at least not for me. His monogamy included strip clubs with the boys; that wasn't my idea of monogamy. We didn't see things at all the same."

Ned agreed, "We almost didn't make it. I had an affair with someone who didn't mean anything, really; it was just a one-time sexual thing. And then Ellen had an affair without ever having sex with the guy, but was emotionally involved with someone who meant a lot to her. We both got a big kick in the head."

Ellen explained how monogamy was different now for both of them: "Our implicit assumptions led us to this place. We never talked about our expectations before getting married; we just assumed that we agreed. I said 'I do,' and then I was saying 'I don't' almost every day after that. Today I realize we have got to redefine this marriage if we are going to make it work at all."

Ned and Ellen's affairs gave them an opportunity to examine their implicit assumptions. They would need to learn to talk about expectations and move toward a new monogamy. Even after three decades of marriage, they believed they could start again with a new vision—of a new marriage.

How Do You Want Your New Relationship to Look?

Before we get to the next chapter, where you will be doing some intensive work to come to some new agreements about your relationship, start thinking about what you really want this time around. This chapter will help you create that vision so that when you begin the dialogue, you'll have a good sense of your ideal relationship going forward.

The affair will have upset many of your long-held beliefs, concerning not only what your marriage was about, but also perhaps even monogamy and relationships in general. You may have spent some time considering what your life would look like if you left your relationship and what it might look like to be in a relationship with somebody else. Maybe you've even spent some time wishing that things could just go back to the way they were.

As mentioned in this book, you now have the opportunity to create a new relationship with your current partner, one where both of your needs—including the needs that weren't being met that may have contributed to the affair—are out in the open. This chapter will help you think about what you want from this new relationship, while the next chapter will lead you and your partner through the process of creating a new monogamy agreement.

Maintaining and Expanding

Relationships, like most of life, are constantly growing and changing. Some people are more comfortable with avoiding change, and as long as things stay the same, they feel happy or at least stable. Other people love the idea of constantly expanding, trying new things and actively changing their lifestyles to reflect their evolving values.

Both styles of being in a relationship have limitations. *Maintainers*—people who tend to avoid change—are stabilizers. They like to keep the peace and find ways to avoid chaos. They are good at finding one thing they like and doing it well, becoming an expert, but they may feel stuck and can find it hard to move forward in their lives because change frequently causes them stress. Maintainers will be happy in a relationship that doesn't expand or grow, even if some parts of it are unsatisfying, because it feels comfortable, and they are unlikely to create or ask for dramatic shifts. *Expanders*—those who seek out change and growth—find new and creative ways to live their lives, always pushing the edge and looking for new things to try. Yet they may find that their wish for excitement and change can create conflict in relationships when they get bored with the status quo and find themselves wanting to move things forward or shake things up. If these two types are in a relationship together, they may find that their different needs and wants in the relationship can be a source of friction and misunderstanding.

Not surprisingly, maintainers and expanders have a way of finding one another and ending up in a relationship together. Maintainers can be attracted to expanders' exciting and vibrant approach to life, and expanders can be attracted to maintainers' stability and balanced viewpoints.

Exercise 4.1   Are You a Maintainer or an Expander?

Here's a simple way to decide whether you are a maintainer or an expander. You can also do this exercise with your partner in mind to determine which type she is. This may help you understand some of the dynamics in your relationship.

Expanders:

Do you often have great ideas for new projects?

Are you a creative person who has plans to start new things much of the time?

Do you start things but sometimes have trouble finishing them?

Do you get bored if things are too consistent and steady in your life?

Do you like to try new foods, make new friends, and have new adventures often?

If you answered yes to most or all five of these questions, you are probably an expander. You are a creative thinker who likes to take risks. You may also find that you have trouble finishing projects or have many unfinished tasks.

Maintainers:

Do you have one thing in which you are an expert or that you specialize in?

Are you really good at something that you put most of your energy into on a regular basis?

Would you rather take the same road home every night?

Are you uncomfortable in new situations or meeting new people?

Do you prefer to stay home and spend time with family and friends doing things that are familiar to you?

If you answered yes to most or all five of these questions, you are probably a maintainer. You are probably very good at what you do and can be counted on to be an expert at whatever you take on. You may also feel stuck and find it difficult to make major changes in your life.

Remember, we need both maintainers and expanders in the world, and you may have some traits of both types. Yet you may also find that some of your frustration with your partner comes from longing for your partner to be more of one or the other.

If you are the expander in the relationship, you may find that you often want to try new things, and you might expect that a partner who loved you would want to try new things too. But if you are a maintainer, you may feel that any change in the terms of your partnership could be a direct threat to the relationship.

As you consider the future of your current relationship, think about what style you are. Are you an expander, who is interested in changing things up out of boredom with the routine? Or are you a maintainer, who needs to feel secure and safe in a predictable and consistent relationship? Knowing your style will help you determine what you want out of your relationship going forward.

If you are a maintainer, you will need to be sure that your new agreement includes ways for you to feel safe with your partner by integrating things that make you feel secure. This may include regularly checking in with your partner every day by phone, e-mail, or text, or making sure that your partner lets you know ahead of time when plans come up that mean meeting new people.

If you're an expander, it means that you'll need to make sure your agreement includes ways that you can continue to feel interested and excited in your relationship, which may mean being sure to plan a new trip or adventure with your partner at least once a month, or trying new sexual activities with your partner regularly.

Old Vows vs. New Vows

As you look back on the vows you made to your partner, would you choose to make them over again? If you look at them and really identify what they mean to you on a deeper level, it's likely that you might decide to make some of them again, but you may want to spend time considering what they really mean to you at this time in your life and in your partnership. If you could, would you create new vows? Before you get into creating your new agreement in the next chapter, it's time to think about what has true meaning for you and your relationship going forward. Sometimes it takes almost losing it all to believe that you can have what you have really always wanted. The discussions and exercises in this chapter will help you explore whether or not your old vows are relevant to your new relationship.

How Promises Can Change

We change as we grow and mature into adults, and our beliefs about relationships change as well. We may keep our promises throughout our lifetimes. Or we might instead believe that our commitments should grow as we grow.

One couple, Mark and Dan, committed to each other when they were in their early twenties. At that time, they promised they would never travel without each other. Mark's job took him on assignment to some faraway and, at times, dangerous places. As he got older, he felt that having Dan with him made him look immature to his colleagues, who thought he was afraid of traveling alone. He also thought that Dan was getting bored during these trips and relied too heavily on Mark to entertain him at night when Mark was often tired after long days on the road. They decided that their agreement had to change.

They didn't talk about it at first, and Mark just arbitrarily started making reservations when Dan wasn't available. He slowly started changing the rules, and their relationship began to unravel. Dan thought Mark was having an affair, and he began to feel disconnected. Dan confronted Mark and told him how he felt using "I" statements: "I sense that you are changing the rules, which makes me feel that you are abandoning me, leaving me behind when you travel. We used to do all this stuff together. It seems obvious that you're cheating on me, and I want to know what's going on with you."

Instead of arguing or lying to Dan about how he felt, Mark told Dan the truth: that he wanted to change their agreement. At first Dan thought this meant that Mark wanted to have other sexual partners on the road and was looking for more freedom. Mark told him that he did want more freedom, that he was expanding into a new developmental stage of his life, but that it had nothing to do with his sexuality, only his independence as an individual. He told Dan he wanted to start traveling alone for work and to explore what that felt like. Dan asked if Mark could stay closely connected to him when he traveled through VoIP (Internet phone or video chat) and texting. Mark agreed and said it would help him feel connected as well.

Mark and Dan shifted their agreement when it became clear that it wasn't working for Mark and that his decisions were negatively affecting Dan. Mark might have spoken to Dan earlier about his growing unease with having Dan travel everywhere with him, but he was uncomfortable doing so. However, when Dan spoke to him about the changes he noticed in the relationship, Mark was relieved to have everything out in the open, and both men were able to agree on changes in their relationship that would allow them to stay connected while also meeting their individual needs.

Even though Dan did miss traveling with Mark, eventually he began to meet new friends that he enjoyed connecting with and who helped him grow past his need to be with Mark at all times. Both partners enjoyed their newfound independence, and though both had been somewhat worried that so much time apart would destabilize their relationship, they grew closer when they changed their agreement to allow for more room for each to pursue his life outside their relationship.

Challenging Your Old Beliefs

Because of the affair, what you have believed until now about relationships has shifted in some fundamental way. Your trust in your partner has been challenged. Maybe what you believed about partnerships in general has also changed in some deep and life-changing ways.

You now have the chance to challenge your implicit monogamy assumptions, and to choose to recreate your monogamy in ways that align with your true beliefs and desires. This is your chance to create a new relationship with new expectations. And this time, you can share your expectations openly with your partner and talk about how to do your new marriage differently.

Passion and Connection

We all desire a passionate and connected relationship. This seems to be a universal longing. No matter what the culture or society, most of us want to form a pair-bond with someone, whether we're young, old, or somewhere in between. Those who don't seek partnerships are seen as outside the norm. Yet some of us risk those committed partnerships for brief erotic flings and sexual and emotional entanglements. It's important to acknowledge that the personal challenges around creating fidelity can make marriage one of the most difficult, if not the very hardest, goal of your entire lifetime.

But it can be worth it. Having a passionate relationship and desire for your spouse creates amazing amounts of energy, both in your relationship and for each of you individually. It gives hope for the future, restores self-esteem, and energizes other parts of life as well: work, family, and creative pursuits. There seems to be nothing more important. For many of us, creating a fidelity agreement with a partner where there is erotic energy, passion, and nurturing energy is the ultimate goal of our lives.

Affairs can bring back passion. One reason why people have affairs is that they long for a feeling of passion and creativity that they may not feel in the primary relationship. They want the vitality of an intimate connection, and when they don't feel this in their current relationships, they may seek out a new partner who gives them a sense of connection, erotic passion, or the emotional understanding that they're missing.

Infidelity can be an effort to reclaim a self-identity as a sexual being, as someone worth loving or valued by another. If your partner, for whatever reason, wasn't feeling this way in your relationship, this may have been why he strayed. It's important in the new monogamy that you and your partner include agreements that will help you both feel wanted, loved, and sexually vital with one another, as well as with others, if you choose to open your relationship to that possibility.

Exercise 4.2   What Makes You Feel Alive?

What are some of the things that make you feel alive and vital in a relationship? Take a moment to note in your journal a few of the things that make you feel passionate and energized. Brainstorming here will help you clarify what you want in your new monogamy agreement as you move into the next chapters. Here are some questions to ask yourself:

What do I need to feel good about myself on a daily basis?

What do I need from a partner to feel good in my relationship?

What makes me feel most alive?

What makes me feel passionate when I am with a lover?

What makes me feel vital and important in the world?

These are big questions. Take the time to answer them in more than a few words. They may be short essays or even short stories, as you think about what makes you feel most alive in your life and in your body, mind, and spirit. The following is another approach.

Complete the following statements, without thinking too hard or judging your words. Write down the first thing that comes to your mind:

I am…

I love…

I need…

When you are done with your lists and feel comfortable, read them out loud to your partner. You may notice that they read like a beautiful poem. They are the poetry of your spirit. You could do this exercise every day, and the list would be different each time. For today, this is your personal spirit poem. Save your lists in a special place. Remember to have compassion for yourself, and don't judge yourself for the things you need and love.

Integrate the new people that you are. When partners cheat, they re-create themselves, opening up to a new part of the personality that comes alive with the affair partner. Your partner may feel like a different person mirrored in the affair partner's eyes. This new person may cause your partner to feel more confident, sexier, smarter, more charming; all of the things your partner felt during the affair became a part of her personality when she was with the affair partner. Once that new self is created, it may be difficult to turn off or deny after the affair is over.

Similarly, partners who were cheated on will have changed as well. They may become less trusting or, on the other hand, discover new inner strength. In either case, your new, shared vision of the future will have to include these new parts of yourselves. You will have to integrate the more self-confident, sexier, more experienced, and tougher selves into your new relationship together.

If denied, these new parts of your personalities will go underground and resurface later, or you will feel as if parts of you are split off from the new relationship that you are trying to create together.

Exercise 4.3   How Have You Changed?

Some questions to ask yourself to help you pinpoint what parts of you have been developed as a result of the affair are as follows. Take a moment to think about what you were like before the affair and what you are like now. This is a difficult exercise in self-discovery. You may want to ask your partner to help you. Chances are your partner can help you identify ways that you have changed since the affair, for better and for worse.

Since the affair…

I have changed for the better in that now I…

I have changed for the worse in that now I…

One thing I have discovered about myself is…

Something I realized about myself is…

A new part of myself that I have discovered is…

One new thing I feel about myself is…

One way I notice that I act now is…

Creating a New Vision of the Relationship

The next few chapters include some growth exercises that will help you explore your desires and longings. One way to grow together as a couple is to share longings in safe ways. True relationship happens when you can stretch toward what your partner desires from you. In this way, you can grow as a partner and as an individual. And growing fully as a sexual partner leads to full growth as an emotional, physical, and spiritual person.

In the next chapter, you'll have frank discussions about what you and your partner desire from the relationship, including explicitly stating what sort of fidelity you will expect from one another. It's possible that one or both of you may be curious about having a relationship that is more fluid than traditional monogamy, or neither of you might want this.

But to explore your options, you'll need to understand what those options are. Next, I've listed some types of relationships, from fully closed monogamy to a fully open marriage. As you read, notice whether you are drawn to any of these relationship types, and if so, what draws you to them. If you're curious about having a semi-open relationship, for example, what about it piques your curiosity? Is it the idea of being able to have a new lover occasionally, or simply the thought of being able to look at and flirt with other potential lovers even if you don't think you'd ever really want anyone besides your partner as a lover? Right now you're only thinking about these things, so it doesn't do any harm to consider these options, even if in the end, you and your partner decide to stick with traditional forms of monogamy.

Options for Your New Relationship

The new monogamy happens on a continuum, from totally closed to totally open. Part of the new monogamy is consciously and explicitly exploring where your new relationship will exist on the monogamy continuum, at least initially (discussed in the next chapter).

Your new relationship will continue to grow and change as each of you grows and changes, and it may change position on the continuum throughout the years. However, the initial agreement that you create will offer you a place to start on the continuum, from which you can continue to negotiate your agreements going forward. The following are the most common types of relationships on the monogamy continuum. Keep in mind that you and your partner can decide on anything that works for both of you, from a combination of these options to something entirely new.

Closed Marriage

This option, of course, is what most of us think of when we think of "monogamy." A closed marriage is one where the partners have agreed to only have sexual and emotional connection with one another for as long as they are together. This book has covered some of the rewards of this type of marriage. A closed marriage, like all agreements, can suffer from the effects of unspoken implicit assumptions, and can benefit from having each partner's expectations about marriage brought into the open. Even if you choose to keep your marriage closed, you may decide to have certain options open for discussion along the way.

Semi-open Relationship

The rest of the continuum will necessarily involve various levels of openness. If we define "monogamy" as not just synonymous with a closed marriage, but as a commitment to emotional fidelity to one another based on a monogamy agreement, then the new monogamy is about the right to decide, as a couple, how open you want your relationship to be.

A semi-open relationship means that there is an agreement that there can be emotional or possibly even sexual connections with others outside of the relationship, but these connections are carefully controlled and are subject to restrictions.

For instance, a couple may decide that they can "play" sexually with others, but only if both partners are together. Or it may mean that the partners are allowed to explore online sexual or emotional connections, but that these relationships can't be brought into the "face-to-face" world.

Some couples agree that they can kiss or fondle others, but their rule is that they are not allowed to have intercourse or other types of sex, and all of this happens only when they are with one another. Obviously there are as many potential semi-open relationships as there are couples. Whatever you both decide is the right decision for you and your partner.

Open Marriage

Open marriage is a marriage with rules chosen by the couple that leave options open to develop outside sexual relationships. "Open marriage" is a general term that covers a myriad of possibilities. Couples describe themselves as being in an open marriage when they feel open to more sexual possibilities than in closed marriages, or when they are willing to have sexual experiences with other people besides their partners and it is accepted as part of their monogamy agreement.

Some couples in open marriages take their relationships on a case-by-case basis, deciding as they go along what to do about their desire to take things outside the marriage. The key element is that they discuss all possibilities and that the feelings of both partners are relevant and determine what will take place.

This type of relationship includes negotiating sexual relationships on the side that are out in the open so that a partner never feels compelled to lie. In these types of marriages, couples can have sexual connections with others as long as there is complete honesty and disclosure.

Open marriage involves a more fluid idea of connection to the primary partner. The primary partner remains the main attachment, and the secondary relationship happens without negatively affecting the marriage. This, as you may imagine, can be complicated, yet for some couples, the transparency helps them feel more confident. There's no need to worry about lying or cheating if everything is out in the open.

Some couples who have solid relationships and can talk openly and freely about their arrangements can live for years in open marriages, taking on outside sexual partners while staying connected primarily and foremost to one another.

Polyamory

Polyamory—from the Greek *poly*, meaning "many," and the Latin *amor*, meaning "love"—simply means "many loves." "Polyamory" is not a legal term, as in *polygamy*, which means being married to more than one spouse.

Polyamory is different from open marriage in that it differentiates between mere sex for fun with outside partners, and loving, emotional connections outside the marriage bond. Polyamory differs from open marriage in that outside relationships are based on emotional connections, not just sex. "Poly" couples distinguish themselves from "swingers," for whom sex is just for fun. Poly couples believe that we can love more than one person at a time and that we can maintain a primary partner and still love a secondary partner.

Polyamory is growing in popularity in the United States, for both men and women, gay and straight, who are identifying themselves more and more as preferring a nontraditional relationship lifestyle. In a 2009 *Newsweek* article, journalist Jessica Bennett writes that "…openly polyamorous families in the United States number more than half a million…with thriving contingents in nearly every major city."

Many couples find that polyamory is a unique way of dealing with the desire for long-term commitment *and* the desire for new relationship energy. To some, polyamory may sound challenging, and to others it may be the answer to the difficulties of long-term monogamy.

Polysexuality

Polysexual experiences are different from polyamorous relationships, in that polyamorous relationships center on emotional connection and bonding. *Polysexuality*, on the other hand, is a way to describe couples or individuals who experience multiple types and ways of having sex. Polysexuality is about having sexual experiences outside of your primary relationship, with the understanding that deeper emotional connection is reserved for the primary partner. This type of relationship may or may not include rules about being open. The couple negotiates secrecy versus privacy, where some details may be kept private from the primary partner to avoid hurt. Yet the open nature of the relationship is such that each partner understands that sexual experiences will be explored at will. Some people say that they don't "own" a partner's body, and want the person to experience pleasure in any way desirable, even without them.

In the past polysexuality was similar to swinging. "Swingers" traditionally were couples who swapped partners for a sexual experience, or shared purely erotic fun with other couples. Polysexual couples today are deciding the rules of their monogamy freely and with fewer restrictions than other open couples.

Exercise 4.4   Thinking More about What You Want

As you read about each of these options—closed, semi-open, open, polyamory, and polysexuality—what came up for you? Since these may be options for you to discuss in your new monogamy agreement, take a moment to consider seriously what you might want and what you don't want in your marriage. Think about each type of relationship, and respond to these areas with your first thoughts:

Closed Marriage

My fears: _____

My worries: _____

My desires: _____

Semi-open Marriage

My fears: _____

My worries: _____

My desires: _____

Open Marriage

My fears: _____

My worries: _____

My desires: _____

Polyamorous Marriage

My fears: _____

My worries: _____

My desires: _____

Polysexual Marriage

My fears: _____

My worries: _____

My desires: _____

Share your thoughts with your partner, and have your partner share his thoughts with you when you are both ready to talk about your new relationship.

It's Only Open Marriage before an Affair

"Finding emotional and erotic satisfaction with multiple partners is our birthright, isn't it? Who's to tell us we shouldn't love more than one person?" said Julia, thirty-six-year-old mother of two. She sat in my office and talked to me about her relationships with her boyfriend, Jasper, and her husband, Lawrence.

"I want it, and I want it for my husband. It's just not easy," she said. "I look at my neighbors, and they are all cheating on each other. It's not easy on them either. So who has it better? I, who can sleep with whom I want, love whom I want, bring home whom I want? I'm not lying to my husband; he knows where I am at night. Or does my neighbor have it better? She's sitting up right now, wondering where her husband is because he comes home late from work. He will tell her he's been at the office, but you and I and *she* know he's lying. It's hard, for sure. We fight. We get jealous. But we'd do that anyway. This way it's all out in the open. It's one less thing to make you crazy."

Before an affair, an open marriage may seem like a way to avoid betrayal. But even couples in open marriages can cheat. If you have promised to be monogamous to your husband and to have only one lover on the side, you can still cheat on both of them by not living up to the agreements you've made with each of them. Open marriage does not guarantee honesty, nor is it a preventive against infidelity. It's simply another type of monogamy agreement, and it works for some people.

In an open relationship, transparency must become the rule. If you attempt to create an open marriage or relationship, transparency will need to be the most important aspect of your monogamy agreement. As you strive to maintain intimacy with your partner, you will need to work on creating an ongoing intimate and emotional attachment, using the tools in this book and other resources if necessary, to reestablish trust with and commitment to one another.

On the other hand, if an open marriage is simply an excuse for your partner to continue the infidelity with your permission, perhaps the idea of open marriage isn't really about the desire to be with you at all.

Having an open marriage is not an excuse to cheat. Having open rules is not just giving each other the right to cheat. And, particularly after an affair, it can feel scary to give your partner permission to seek out other lovers. One important thing to consider is that it's not an open marriage if one of you is already cheating. That is, asking for permission for something you're already doing is, in effect, dishonest. Breaking an agreement and then asking for permission to continue after the damage has already been done is not creating an open and honest relationship. Don't allow your partner to justify continuing the affair by calling it an open marriage. This is not really a negotiation for a new monogamy. This is just a way to justify old behavior. Be very clear with your partner (and yourself) that you will not be manipulated into including the affair partner in your marriage. This arrangement has to work for both of you or neither of you.

If you feel pressured by your partner to open up your relationship and you aren't sure that this is what you want, consider seeing an open-minded couples therapist who can help you explore the idea. If your partner isn't willing to take your concerns into consideration, you may be better off moving on.

In this chapter, you explored some of your needs, desires, worries, and fears about developing a new relationship with your current partner. What you have learned about yourself and your desires will enable you to move forward with a clearer sense of the transformations you will need to see in your relationship to make it work.

In the next chapter, you will create your new monogamy agreement. By now, you've learned a great deal. You will be clearer about what you want in your new relationship. And you will be ready to move forward into creating your new monogamy agreement. You are now ready to cocreate a new monogamy agreement that works for both of you.

CHAPTER 5

Creating a New Monogamy Agreement

To create a new relationship that serves both of you, you must each be explicit about what you need, while considering your partner's vision of what monogamy might look like. The new monogamy is a relationship committed to this shared vision; together, you will work toward fulfilling one another's deepest desires.

In the last chapter, you explored your personal wishes for your new relationship. In this chapter, we will look at expanding your vision of this new relationship through a dialogue with your partner and working to create one mutual, explicit agreement that will define the behaviors you each want within your new relationship.

What Are Monogamy Agreements?

Monogamy agreements are just what they sound like: the explicit agreements you and your partner discuss and choose based on each of your individual needs within the relationship. A monogamy agreement can mean agreeing that you will have a traditional monogamous relationship: no sexual or emotional connections aside from one another. Or, it can mean that you can both have outside lovers. It may mean that you agree that you have sexual relationships with people online or that you can each only admire others from afar.

Your monogamy agreement may stipulate that you are encouraged to tell your partner about other people you desire, as a way to spice up your relationship. You may decide to share sexual experiences online. Or you may agree that it's acceptable to form sexual or emotional bonds with outside people, within certain limits. Those limits might include very specific rules around outside relationships, such as agreeing that your primary relationship is your first priority. Your agreement can include anything on the monogamy continuum.

Monogamy agreements are an obligation that you willingly step into each day as a way to support your relationship and meet both your own and your partner's needs. Like the original and perhaps more "standard" monogamy agreement that you made when you got married, any agreement you make in your relationship should be of the highest priority. If at any time, you are tempted to break the new agreement, this is an issue you need to discuss with your spouse. Talking about your fears and temptations is the beginning of changing how you relate to one another in your new relationship.

As discussed earlier in this book, each of you may have very different implicit understandings of your agreement. Never assume that you automatically understand each other's inner fantasies and desires. This chapter will walk you through how to discuss them and make them explicit.

As you learned from the agreement you made when you first committed to your partner, monogamy agreements are developmental in nature and change over time. Either one or both of you thought you had agreed to sexual and emotional fidelity to your partner for as long as you were together (or even perhaps for as long as you were both to live). Then one, or possibly even both, of you went against that agreement. The agreement shifted. As you and your partner change and grow, it's entirely possible that your new agreement will change as well. By working through the process set forth in this book, this time you won't be surprised by this shifting, but will understand that this is a normal part of the development of a relationship and that you can discuss these shifts with your partner at every turning point.

We will talk more about how to keep your agreements current later in this chapter; it's important that you check in with each other regularly about whether your new monogamy agreement is still working for both of you.

Will Your New Agreement Cause More Problems Than It Solves?

After an affair has affected your relationship, the thought of changing the rules to allow for more fluidity may seem as if it could only create more instability. It might feel as if the two of you were creating a slippery slope that could lead to another betrayal or the end of your relationship altogether.

For some couples, this may certainly be true. An affair may signify that you actually need to create more exclusive time together to reestablish trust and intimacy before even considering other options. This is why the idea of evolving agreements is so crucial to the new monogamy. As you discovered via the affair, your lives are constantly changing, and so are your expectations and needs from your relationship. This chapter will help you create the new monogamy agreement that works for you, and later, as you revisit and tweak the agreement, you can make any changes that seem appropriate.

How do you know what kind of agreement would strengthen your marriage and what kind might derail it? Is there a way to find out before you embark on this new monogamy? These are questions that most couples ask themselves when they begin this journey of exploring options in the marriage or committed relationship. The first step in answering these questions is to bring your fears out into the open.

Now is the time to discuss all your fears about your relationship and your future, and the dialogue techniques in this book (including exercise 5.1, "Practice the New Vision Dialogue," later in this chapter) are some important tools for doing that. Feel free to have a dialogue at any time during the process of creating your new agreement and afterward, as you revisit that agreement. You can use the new vision format or choose another approach that works for you when discussing your issues, fears, and worries with your partner. And please know that it's normal for any tension or problems in your relationship that were there prior to the affair to surface at this point.

The strength of the foundation of your relationship will determine what it can withstand as you push its limits, if you decide to create an agreement that is more fluid than traditional monogamy. The process of discussing your relationship will help you learn to use more-open dialogue skills and a new way of talking about your relationship, which will also help you when you come across issues that arise with your new agreement. This is an important part of establishing a strong relationship foundation. Continuing to talk about your fears and your feelings throughout the lifetime of your marriage or partnership is the only way to avoid misunderstanding, resentment, or, worse, a breach in your monogamy agreement.

Rob and Melissa had been married for six years when they came to me for therapy to help them with their affair recovery. Melissa had recently discovered that Rob had been cheating with their next-door neighbor, Michelle, for well over a year. After Rob was caught, Melissa tearfully admitted to Rob that she, too, had had a brief fling. Her fling had been with a coworker and had lasted for three months. She told Rob that the workplace affair had begun and ended right after she and Rob had become engaged.

These were shocking revelations for both Rob and Melissa, and led to some intense conversations about their relationship, their denial, and their mutual dishonesty. They realized that they each felt hurt and betrayed but that even with all of the intense feelings, they still loved one another.

After some consideration, they decided they wanted to stay together and work on developing a new relationship. They decided that their new monogamy would mean a new type of partnership in which neither of them had to lie to one another to get their needs met.

This new honesty started in therapy. They each admitted that their affairs had been exciting, erotic, and more intense than their own sexual relationship had been in recent years.

They started to discuss what a new monogamy might look like going forward, and explored all options in these discussions. They talked about the possibility of sharing sex partners, but when it came down to it, both Rob and Melissa were really uncomfortable with the idea of fully opening their marriage.

At the same time, they realized that they both had gained enjoyment, excitement, and a deeper experience of their own relationship from their affairs.

They had continued to have sex with each other even during the affairs. It seemed that they both had used their affairs to intensify their sexual experiences together, bringing the erotic energy home to each other. They said the sex was hotter at home when they were sneaking around outside. At first this was incredibly painful and difficult for both of them to hear. Yet as the therapy developed, both Rob and Melissa were more open and honest about their feelings for one another than they had ever been. They each admitted openly that the sex had been amazing when the other partner was cheating.

"I knew something was going on," said Melissa, "because Rob was always wanting to have sex with me, and in new and kinky ways. I kind of suspected he might be fooling around, but frankly—I'm almost ashamed to say—I liked the intensity at home, so I never asked him about it. I look back now and think maybe I was even into it a little. The thought of him with someone else might have turned me on a little. Don't get me wrong: it was devastating emotionally, but that didn't stop me from wanting to have sex with him."

They were curious about how to make it acceptable within the marriage to have sexual experiences with other partners, but they wanted to make sure their relationship with one another stayed safe and secure.

When they came to me, they were interested in forging a new monogamy agreement that would include the possibility of other sexual partners, but they weren't sure how to proceed and were still hurting from the discovery of their affairs.

Rob and Melissa had to grieve the ending of the relationship they had thought they had, even though both of them admitted that the relationship hadn't felt vibrant for many years except, ironically, for the times when they were each with someone else.

Their work consisted of letting go of the old vision of their relationship, learning to trust one another again, and going through the process of creating new explicit agreements about their relationship that would serve the needs and desires of both of them.

Discussing the New Monogamy

Sitting down with your partner and beginning a conversation about a new monogamy will be difficult. An affair can make you realize how far apart you and your partner really are in the vision of what monogamy looks like. Maybe you tried to talk about your issues initially, after the discovery of the affair, but have given up in frustration or discomfort. You may have even tried couples counseling and found that these conversations opened up a Pandora's box of questions and painful issues. You may now feel like avoiding the topic at all costs, simply because talking about it can be so painful.

However, now that one or both of you has cheated, you are at the point in your relationship where change has to happen for you to move forward. It's vital that you now open up the conversation so that you can clear up any confusion between you about the nature of your commitment.

Later in this chapter is a questionnaire designed to get you and your partner thinking in detail about your needs and desires in several areas of your relationship. Throughout the chapter, you'll find questions that you and your partner might choose to use in a formal dialogue or casually, as you continue to discuss what your relationship will look like going forward. You can use these questions as a way to begin your new monogamy conversation now and later, as your monogamy agreement evolves. Given that you are reading this book, you are ready to set some new boundaries and try a new way of being together. Hopefully your partner is ready too. For many couples, this can be an exciting (and scary) time.

Exercise 5.1   Practice the New Vision Dialogue

Chapter 2 introduced the Imago dialogue technique, which is a way to discuss intense emotional issues in a simple and structured way that helps both people feel heard. In the following dialogue, you'll focus on discussing how you want your relationship to look as you move forward. Remember that one of you will be the sender (speaker), and the other will be the receiver (listener). The sender will complete the following sentence stems, and the receiver will use mirroring (repeating back what the sender said), validation (offering understanding of the sender's experience), and empathy (offering an understanding of how the sender might be feeling or has felt). Refer back to chapter 2 if you need a refresher in creating this dialogue.

Choose a time when both of you have at least one uninterrupted hour. Turn off the phone, and limit any other distractions, such as the children, pets, television, the computer, or pressing chores. You may not have time to cover everything in one session, and that's fine. You may need to do this several times over a couple of weeks. Remember that you can also use this technique any time either of you feels the need to discuss a difficult topic. For now, focus on what you both want out of your new post-affair relationship.

The two of you can create any dialogue you want, improvising, as long as both partners feel heard and acknowledged. Keep the focus of the dialogue on the new relationship agreement you wish to create with your partner, and if the conversation begins to turn into an argument, it's fine to agree to revisit it later or to take five or ten minutes to calm down before continuing. Use this process in a way that feels comfortable to you.

If you are the receiver, you don't have to agree, disagree, explain, or make promises to the sender. You are just trying to understand the sender's point of view and where she is coming from. Can you help the sender feel understood? Can you really see her side of the situation and get clear on what she is experiencing? If you can, you never have to argue. If you can validate each other's experience, there's nothing to prove. You can stop trying to convince each other that your experience is the "right" way to feel. Both of you have your own experiences, and each is valid.

Common Issues with the Dialogue

During the dialogue, when you are the receiver, if you become triggered and feel the need to react, see if you can hold off on expressing
these feelings and just stay focused on your partner. Mirror your partner,
and hold back on your own reactions for now. You will get your turn too.
But for now, don't make it about you; let the focus stay on your partner,
and simply mirror him and try to understand his perspective. The only
time the dialogue should break this structure is if the sender becomes
cruel or abusive. You don't have to sit still and mirror someone who is
calling you names or being hurtful on purpose. Yes, some things your
partner says may hurt, but that's different from when your partner purposely says things that are meant to wound you.

If your partner seems to be saying things that are intended to hurt,
you can ask him to be more sensitive to your feelings, or you can
choose to end the dialogue and revisit it later with the agreement that
neither of you attacks, abuses, or intentionally wounds the other. If you
can't seem to stop attacking one another, you might consider having a
couples therapist help you explore your new monogamy agreement.

New Vision Dialogue

Sender.   One thing I appreciate about being in a relationship with
             you is _____ .

Receiver. [Mirror.]

Sender.   One way I can see monogamy in our new relationship
             might be _____ .

Receiver. [Mirror.]

Sender.   One way I might be frightened of this would
             be _____ .

Receiver. [Mirror.]

Sender. What I can do to move in the direction of this new monogamy is _____ .

Receiver. [Mirror.]

Sender. One way you could help me would be _____ .

Receiver. [Mirror.]

Validation

Receiver. Knowing you, I can understand that you _____ , because _____ .

Empathy

Receiver. It makes sense that you feel _____ , because _____ .

Appreciation

Receiver. One thing I appreciated about this dialogue was _____ .

Sender. One thing I appreciated about this dialogue was _____ .

Now switch roles and repeat.

This dialogue will allow you both to explore your relationship more deeply and to be truly honest about what you want to happen in the future. Once you have both been the sender and the receiver, you may want to take some time to reflect on what came out of the dialogue. Were there things that came up that surprised you or your partner about your own or your partner's vision of the relationship? Were there things that made one or both of you uncomfortable? If so, take the time to write down your feelings about these emotions. You will address them later, when you create your new agreement.

Discussing Your Fears and Worries

Based on what came up in the previous dialogue, you or your partner may have heard some difficult truths about how one or both of you feel or want to change the relationship, or about what happened during the affair. This means that you both are being truly honest, perhaps for the first time in a long time or ever, about your vision for the relationship.

For instance, if one partner shares that she's interested in Internet-only intimate relationships with others, it may trigger all kinds of feelings for the partner who never even considered that his partner might want such a thing. These feelings may include anger, fear, and resentment, or even feelings of intrigue, curiosity, and excitement.

Exercise 5.2   Continuing Your Dialogue

Using the previous dialogue process, take turns revealing any fears you have about changing your monogamy agreement. Some initial fears might be:

"Will our relationship really survive if we change the rules?"

"Can we change our relationship so that we can have a more fluid definition of monogamy and still stay connected to each other?"

"If I change to give you what you want, aren't you just going to keep asking me to give more and more?"

"What if we try something new and I don't like it? Can we change back?"

"What if we start a new kind of monogamy and you still cheat on me?"

"What if we open our marriage and I don't fall back in love with you?"

"What if I want to stay friends with my lover and you say it's okay, but you are really harboring secret resentment, never really forgive me, and just hold it against me?"

You get the idea. We all have fears whenever our relationships change. The difference this time is that you will discuss your fears, bringing them up whenever they surface. The important thing is to take responsibility for them yourself, without blaming your partner for your feelings or making him responsible for your unhappiness.

Exercise 5.3   Making Sense of Your Fears

As you and your partner dig into the deeper meanings of each other's fears, you can begin to uncover what's truly happening. This conversation may awaken both of you to some deeper issues that can bring you closer to each other and to some of the things that might even have stopped the affair from happening if you had been able to discuss them prior to the infidelity.

Similarly, you can use this dialogue format to explore the positive things that you both hope might come out of creating your new monogamy agreement, whether or not you decide to create a more fluid arrangement than you had before the affair. You can use "I" statements, such as "My fantasy is that I will _____ or you will _____."

Here are some questions you might ask one another:

"How would a new agreement change our relationship for the better?"

"How could a new agreement bring us closer?"

"How could a new agreement bring us a more intimate emotional relationship with one another?"

When Rob and Melissa used this dialogue process, Rob acknowledged that he fantasized about being able to explore aspects of his sexuality with other people. He wanted to try things that Melissa had never been interested in. He also wanted to know that he would still be able to come home to Melissa, whom he considered the love of his life. Acknowledging this fantasy while acknowledging the importance of Melissa in his life made him realize that what he really wanted was to try those things with Melissa, not other women. Sharing this actually lessened Melissa's fear that Rob was looking for another woman to fill her place.

Although Melissa still had to deal with her own fears that Rob would leave her if they opened up their marriage, his honesty in this instance helped her understand the depth of his feelings for her. He also was willing to keep the fantasy at a "fantasy only" level if that was what Melissa needed to feel safe. She might never agree to open up their marriage, but she now had a new perspective on Rob's feelings for her and a new understanding of her own fears. Melissa mirrored Rob's statement back to him several times, so that she could really hear and take in what he was saying, that he wasn't looking to replace her.

Important Topics to Discuss

When creating your new monogamy agreement, it's important to avoid making empty promises. Remember, you both made promises in the past and proved that promises can be broken. The new monogamy is a living vow. A living vow is an action that you take every day, a way of life, rather than simply empty words that you say to placate a hurt or angry partner. A vow is a way to envision your relationship going forward. The following are some things to think about when creating your living vow. Consider your answers and jot them down in your journal. You may refer back to them later, when you are forming your monogamy agreement.

"How might we live our relationship in a way that works for both of us?"

"How might we choose to share our intimate lives, regardless of what others think?"

"What is right for us now, and how can we include new rules as we change and grow?"

"Can we make sure that we have fluidity and variety, but also safety, so that we don't become rigid or anxious?"

Desires, Not Demands

Whenever we talk about our monogamy wishes, we are really talking about our desires, our fantasies, and our vision for a new relationship. And it's entirely likely that much of what you desire will be integrated into your new relationship if you can empathize with each other about what's important.

However, it's up to you to explain to each other why a particular issue is important to your vision. If you demean your partner in the process or express judgment about her concerns, she will see them as more of a demand than a request.

Try not to use this as an opportunity to convince your partner to give you what you want. What's most important is that none of your monogamy desires be seen as a way to manipulate your partner. You don't want your partner to feel as if you were saying "Either you do this, or I'm ending the marriage." That type of either-or message is abusive at best. A marriage or committed partnership must be based on agreed-upon values. Of course, both of you should try to push your own comfort edge and be willing to grow into some new areas, as a way of being generous to your partner.

Yet if you are doing anything because it feels like an ultimatum, this change won't last or be satisfying, ultimately, to either of you. You want your partner to want to create a new relationship with you that is based on mutual decision making. This is not compromise; compromise means that both of you lose something. Rather, it is rooted in a desire to see your partner happy and fulfilled, to be happy and fulfilled yourself, and to know that your partner wants this same thing.

Negotiating Your New Agreement

To begin the work on your new agreement, either alone or with your partner, answer the questions in each section of the following exercise. Honesty is the most important goal here, so make that your priority. You may feel that some things are still too delicate or sensitive when you open your discussion. However, try not to underestimate your partner. If your partner is choosing to continue the relationship with you, he may be more open to hearing your truth than you give him credit for. Remember, these are desires, not demands.

Know that nothing is written in stone. You can always change your mind later. Take as long as you need to answer the questions. When you have your answers, sit down with your partner and review each of your responses together. You may want to use your answers to the questionnaire to create a longer agreement that later may even become written vows. You can use these vows in a recommitment or partnership ceremony, if you wish. However, don't worry too much about that now. Use this exercise as a way to form your conversation about how you want your new relationship to be today.

The following exercise is designed to make you think. You may be surprised by your own or your partner's answers, and even find yourself rethinking monogamy in general. You may also find that the questions make you anxious. You will likely find that you and your partner answer these questions differently. This is completely normal. If strong issues come up that keep you from continuing, ask for a break or a dialogue about those issues, and come back to the questionnaire later. Remember, this is an ongoing conversation that is most helpful as a stepping-stone to ongoing commitment.

The questionnaire is divided into categories, all of which should be covered in your new monogamy agreement. There may be other categories, questions, and areas that aren't covered here. Feel free to add or subtract as necessary. Skip the questions you can't answer right now and revisit them later.

If you find that you reach an impasse, where you both want something different and neither party is willing to budge, put the agreement aside and see if you can work through your issues first.

If the conflict seems irresolute, it may also be a sign that you have hit the crack in the relationship foundation that needs to be repaired before you move into changes that could threaten the stability of your future. If the issue is too difficult to resolve without help, you may want to table your discussion until you can work it out with your couples therapist.

Conflict is inevitable in all relationships. Believing that a partnership without conflict or problems is ideal can be risky, as this vision contains very little reality. Two humans trying to negotiate the world together will always disagree at some point. This has much less significance than you might imagine. What's important to a successful marriage or relationship is how you resolve your conflicts. If conflict is natural in all of life, then it's up to you as a couple to build your survival skills and to become expert in the navigation of your future rocky waters.

Exercise 5.4 The New Monogamy Questionnaire

Review this questionnaire and consider how you would answer each question. Don't worry so much about how your partner might respond.

Thoughts:

"If I have sexual thoughts about other people, do I share them with you?"

"When I have thoughts of others, when do I reveal them?"

"Is it necessary to share every time I think of someone else?"

"Have I cheated in my heart if I imagine being with someone else?"

"If I fantasize about my neighbor's spouse, should I share it or keep it to myself?"

"Is sharing an interest outside the relationship hurtful or helpful?"

"Do I tell you if I have outside desires, even if I don't act on them?"

"If those thoughts may lead me down a path to acting on them, do I tell you about them?"

"Is it necessary to share with you every time I think of someone else as attractive?"

"If I have a bad thought about you, should I share it?"

"Under what circumstances should I avoid telling you what I'm thinking about others?"

"What things do I want you to avoid telling me?"

Fantasies:

"What if I have fantasies of someone else? Should I share them with you?"

"Should we share fantasies and get off on them together?"

"Should we share fantasies about people of the same sex?"

"Should I share fantasies online?"

"Should we watch porn together?"

"What if I have fantasies of making love with someone else while we're making love? Should I keep them to myself? Would it be hurtful or helpful?"

"What if I fantasize about an ex?"

"What if I fantasize out loud?"

"What if I fantasize about something you won't do?"

"Can I share my fantasies with you during sex?"

Desires:

"What if I desire someone else?"

"What if I want a type of sex that I'm afraid to share?"

"What if I am convinced that you won't like what I like?"

"Do I share what I have liked in the past?"

"Do we commit to acting out each other's sexual and romantic desires? What kind of conversation would that be?"

"How do we share sexual fantasies?"

"How do we talk about what we like?

"How do we talk about what we want more of?"

"How do we talk about what we want to try?"

"What if our desire decreases over time?"

"What if one of us feels more desire than the other?"

Arousal:

"Should we talk about it every time we become aroused?"

"What if I become aroused by someone else?"

"When do we have a discussion about arousal?"

"What if I don't feel aroused when we're together? Should I have sex with you anyway?"

"What if I feel aroused by you? Does that mean we should have sex?"

"How do I know if I am aroused? Do you help me figure that out?"

"How do I tell you if something you do turns me off?"

"What if I get aroused during the day? Do I tell?"

"What if I masturbate in the shower? Do I tell?"

"What if I am aroused when I travel? Do I tell?"

"Should I talk about it if one of my friends turns me on?"

"When do you start talking about it if a friendship is starting to get sexual? How do we begin that conversation?"

"Is it okay to go to strip clubs and get turned on?"

"Is it okay to come home from a strip club turned on and want to have sex?"

"Is it okay to get aroused during a massage and tell you about it?"

Flirtation:

"What are our rules about flirting?"

"Is it okay to flirt with someone at work?"

"How about with each other's friends?"

"Can we flirt while we are together?"

"Can we flirt when we are not with each other?"

"Can we confront each other if we see each other flirting? What would be a safe way to do that?"

"How do we tell each other we are uncomfortable with flirting outside our relationship?"

"How should we flirt with each other?"

Emotion:

"Is it okay if I am attracted and emotionally connected to a friend of the opposite sex?"

"Is it okay to be emotionally connected to friends of the sex to which I'm not attracted?"

"Is it all right if I have emotional relationships that don't include you?"

"How much time can I spend with my friends of the sex to which I'm attracted?"

"Do we have to talk about it every time I see a friend you don't like?"

"Do I have to tell you every time I.e-mail a friend you don't like?"

"Should our e-mails be transparent or private?"

"Should you be friends with this person as well?"

"What is the line between emotional friend and emotional affair?"

"Do I tell you if I'm moving the outside relationship into something more physical? When do we talk about that?"

"Is it okay to spend time with a friend to whom I am emotionally attached?"

"When does it become an emotional affair?"

"Is it fair to share our problems or difficulties with an emotional confidant? Can I share anything about you with that person, or are there limits to what I can share?"

Action:

"What are actions that may be threatening to our monogamy? How do we want to handle that?"

"If I start texting or connecting with a potential new lover on a social network, is it a risk?"

"Can we meet a potential or actual lover for lunch, hobbies, or weekends?"

"Should I share personal issues with the other person while we are together?"

"Can we hold hands?"

"How long is too long for a hug?"

"What if we hug for too long? Should I tell you?"

"What if I feel that my emotional affair is moving in a sexual direction?"

"Can I kiss someone else?"

"When do I tell you that I'm starting to cross the line of our agreement? When I am thinking of crossing it? When I have a fantasy? When I make a phone call or e-mail?"

"What if I see you starting to get into a physical or sexual relationship with someone outside of our relationship? When do I say something, and what do I say?"

Connection:

"If I begin to feel connected to someone, how do I manage that?"

"How do I deal with my own jealousy?"

"How do I deal with your jealousy?"

"What are our specific guidelines for opening the relationship to others?"

"What if I want to be close to someone else without intercourse?"

"What if this person is really important to me?"

"What if I feel that we are soul mates?"

"What if I want to be with the other person more than with you?"

"Does this mean we should break up?"

"How do I know if it's real?"

"What if I develop an Internet relationship with someone and we want to meet?"

"How do I share this with you?"

"How often do you and I discuss our relationship?"

"Do we sleep in the same bed? Separate beds? Separate rooms?"

Sex:

"What happens if you and I don't have sex for a week or a month?"

"Is there anything off limits sexually between you and me?"

"Is there anything off limits sexually between you, me, and another person or couple?"

"How many times a week should you and I have sex? How many times per month?"

"How often do we share our fantasies and desires?"

"Do we watch pornography together? How often? Who picks?"

"Do we watch porn separately? How often? Do we tell each other when we do?"

"Do we participate in sex with other people while we are together? Who initiates this sex?"

"Do we keep the outside relationships? Which ones?"

"Do we have sex in the house if the children are at home?"

"Who initiates taking things into action?"

"How do we talk about it and process it?"

"Will we talk before or after?"

"How often will we try to have adventures?"

"What are the ground rules for having sex with others as a couple or as individuals? Are there places that are off limits (such as our bed)?"

"Are there people or types of people who are off limits?"

"Do we only take action with someone while we are together?"

"Will we participate or watch, or both?"

"What if you or I am traveling? Can we take action then?"

"Should I call you first?"

Love:

"Can we love more than one person at a time?"

"Can I love someone else and still love you?"

"What if I have feelings for someone I used to love? Is that person off limits?"

"Do those feelings get pushed underground, or do we talk about them together?"

"Are they too hurtful to discuss or is it hurtful to keep them secret?"

"Can we talk about our love for others?"

"How do we handle jealousy over the feelings we have for others?"

"Can we be polyamorous?"

[For the partner who had the affair] "Have you let go of your lover? If not, do I want that? Would you be able to do that? Can we talk about that together?"

"What if I still love my ex-spouse, but don't want to be married to that person?"

Detachment:

"If I become detached emotionally from you, how do we talk about it?"

"If I feel detached when we are together, do we talk about it?"

"If I detach from sexual or emotional experiences, can we talk about it?"

"How do we come back together after I detach, and how do we try to reconnect?"

"What if I decide to stop our extramarital adventures, but you do not?"

"When do we decide to detach from each other permanently if things aren't working?"

"How do I get you back when you detach from me?"

"When do we pull the other back when we feel detached?"

"Is it fair to let each other detach occasionally to get some space?"

"When is it needy and when is it normal to crave attachment?"

"How do we come back together to try to reconnect?"

"What is important about having separate lives for each of us?"

"How do we stay independent and still rely on each other?"

Domestic questions:

The division of domestic chores and how you handle domestic life are part of how your monogamy will affect your life. Discussing them will help you avoid resentment and increase your connection.

"How do we divide chores?"

"How do we divide child care?"

"Who handles the money for our combined expenses?"

"How do we handle our household money versus our individual budgets?"

"How often do we see your parents?"

"How often do we see my parents?"

"How often do we see other family members?"

"Do we exercise together? How often?"

"How do we handle preparing food? Who plans the meals?"

These lists are minimal, but they can bring up a lifetime of conversation. Add anything else that you think is important. A whole book can be written about the importance of discussing these issues, in addition to your more personal, intimate commitments.

Add anything else that you think is important. Some examples:

"Do we go to couples therapy? How often?"

"Who initiates the therapy?"

"Do we go to couples retreats or workshops? How often?"

"Where do we live, and when do we move?"

Writing Out Your Agreement

After you've discussed the answers to all of the preceding questions and any other issues that came up during your conversations, you now have the ingredients you need to finalize your new monogamy agreement. Write down your final answers to the questionnaire, the ones you and your partner have both agreed on, and any additional agreements you've discussed that you want to include.

You may realize that there are only a few issues on your lists that you have agreed on. Most items will be issues that you have responded to differently, or you may even disagree with each other. The monogamy issues that you can agree on now will form the foundation of your new relationship.

These shared values may be the most important things to both of you. If there are things you have not agreed on that one or both of you feel are deal breakers, stop and revisit them. Either go back and discuss their meanings, or find a way to continue the discussion. You are not ready to finalize this agreement until that happens. And there's no rush. You don't have a deadline. The goal is to keep the conversation open.

This vision for your monogamy should be described in the present tense, as if it's happening now. This makes the agreement real and is more easily reinforced as you read it out loud. You are already complying with the agreement as you create it. It's already a force in your life. Here's an example: "We are having sex once a week. We are open to trying new things. We are talking about it immediately when one of us wants to have sex with someone else. We are discussing it before, during, and after, and processing the feelings of each of us, including jealousy."

The document can be as long or short as you want, but it should cover all of the categories in the previous questionnaire.

Keep in mind that some couples start out very slowly, for instance, at first only agreeing to behaviors that seem nonthreatening. Later they may want to renegotiate the agreement as they become more comfortable with the idea of creating a completely new type of relationship. Slowly they may allow for outside sexual or emotional exploration.

You may decide to agree that you can both flirt with others, but only while you are together. You might include in your agreement that you can't do anything further than that yet. Or you might agree that kissing someone else at a party is okay, but sex is not. Or you may decide that flirting at a party is fine but communicating with that person afterward is not. Discussing these possible scenarios may seem like fantasy that may never become reality. However, it's better to talk about your expectations before anything happens than to have conflict after a problem comes up.

Any agreement you make is perfectly acceptable, as long as the needs of both of you are taken into account. If one partner really does want to go farther than the other, it's important to acknowledge that and to commit to a timeline within which to renegotiate the agreement to allow and validate that person's more adventurous desires. This might sound like, "I know it's important to you to be able to open our marriage at some point. Right now I am not comfortable with that. In one year I would like to sit down and have a conversation about where we are in our relationship and how we each feel about that. Would that be acceptable to you?"

In this way, you acknowledge that something is important to your partner and that you will come back and visit the issue again when more time has passed. Both of you will be in a very different place at that time and may want to revise several things in your agreement. You may want to have a more closed marriage or do something that feels more open. The crucial element here is acknowledging and validating your partner's needs while respecting your own.

Finalizing the Agreement

When your new monogamy agreement is written down for both of you, you may want to make it official: date it, sign it, and keep it somewhere safe. Make sure each partner has a copy. Revisit the monogamy agreement any time you are unsure of your commitment; ask your partner to sit down and go over it again. This can help you feel safe in your relationship and also open up new dialogues about your relationship when you are unsure.

Talk about questions that come up as you move forward with your new agreement, and revise the document when needed.

Your new monogamy agreement is one of the most important things you will accomplish in your lifetime. It shouldn't be taken lightly. Give yourselves credit for having a conscious relationship, and congratulate yourselves for moving forward in your relationship.

Written Contracts vs. Verbal Agreements

Some couples like to ritualize the process of creating a new agreement and make it into a ceremony. A friend, family member, or spiritual leader can witness it. For others, being in nature or a sacred space makes the sharing of this commitment seem more binding.

For many couples, thinking about, writing out, and verbally sharing a commitment to monogamy is a deep and binding vow. And for couples that have experienced hurt and betrayal, it can have special meaning: renewal and recommitment.

Give this experience the sacredness and seriousness it deserves. Or play with it if that's more your style. But talk to each other about how you want this process to be. Don't be disappointed because you expected something from the process that you didn't discuss out loud. Don't expect your partner to read your mind and know what you want. As you found in the dialogue and the previous questionnaire, discussing the details of your explicit hopes and expectations can bring you closer, even if it's a difficult conversation. If your relationship is important to you, it's worth it to risk being uncomfortable if it means strengthening your bond.

Creating a Timeline for Revising Your Agreement

It's important to have a plan for how and when you will revisit the agreement. Will you do it at set times, such as every six months or a year? Or will you only do it if one partner strongly needs for the agreement to change? It's best to choose a specific time or span of time, for instance, a specific date each year, such as Valentine's Day or New Year's Day. Or you may want to renew your agreement on your anniversary every year. This way, the partner who may want a revision doesn't bear the entire responsibility for bringing up the difficult conversation of wanting change. This "clause" should be written into the agreement. Put your agreed-upon date for "renewal" on the calendar. Treat it as you would any important date; it's perhaps the most important meeting that you and your partner will ever have.

When you revisit the agreement, use the techniques in this book that appeal to you. You may decide to revisit the previous questionnaire in its entirety or just the sections that seem appropriate. Or you may write your own questions, based on your experiences in the relationship. However you decide to approach revising your agreement, remember that the agreement is meant to be fluid and to evolve over time as you and your partner change.

Also remember that at any time, one or both partners can ask for a change in the agreement if something in it doesn't seem to be working. Especially in the beginning, you may both find that you need to adjust the terms of the agreement based on experiences or unexpected problems that may crop up. This is perfectly normal and, in fact, healthy. The more open and willing you both are to take each other's needs, and your own, into consideration and continue to have the new monogamy conversation, the stronger your relationship will become.

Can You Have Different Needs?

Wanting and liking different things is normal in a relationship. You might love pizza while your partner prefers sushi. You might want or enjoy one activity in bed while your partner prefers another.

These differences have no bearing on whether or not you will enjoy dinner together or be happy in bed. What determines happiness is how you deal with the conflict of wanting two different things. The goal is to be okay as two different people—to have your individual needs, wants, preferences, and experiences—and to still find joy in being together.

Rob and Melissa found some disparities between what they were willing to agree to. Melissa didn't want to know every time Rob felt aroused by another person or what his fantasies were about that person. Yet Rob wanted to be able to share these feelings with Melissa, because it made him feel closer to her. For Melissa, the thought of hearing Rob's every fantasy only renewed her anxiety. Their compromise was that Rob would ask Melissa if it was okay to share a particular thought or fantasy with her, and she would have the chance to say yes or no to this request, depending on her level of anxiety and closeness to Rob at the time. Rob agreed to abide by her answer and not share a fantasy or thought if she was uncomfortable with his doing so. Melissa also asked Rob to make sure he shared his fantasy without telling her specifically who the other woman was. She asked that he keep it generic, for instance, that he was turned on by "a tall woman in a store" or "a waitress."

They did agree that they could each have separate sexual encounters outside of their marriage. Yet, Rob found that he was uncomfortable with the thought of Melissa meeting someone and going home with him without calling Rob first. Melissa didn't want to have to call Rob; it made her feel awkward and guilty. They compromised by agreeing that once a month, they'd both have a free weekend in which they could do whatever they wanted, including having sexual experiences with others without needing to let the other know. The rest of the month, they would only be with each other.

They decided that they would revisit this aspect of the agreement after three months, to see how each felt about it. The idea of Melissa being with someone else without his knowledge still bothered Rob. And Melissa wasn't sure the agreement would work for her either, because she wondered if their relationship was strong enough to withstand the tension it could create.

Both Melissa and Rob agreed that working out these issues between them could allow them to become closer to one another if they were able to talk about and process their feelings. Hiding from each other and avoiding discussion would probably end their marriage. They committed to listen and respond to one another with respect, and to suspend judgment and criticism.

Sexuality is an extremely sensitive topic for most people. Talking to your partner about your feelings and fears can be a risk. Hearing what your partner considers important about sex can create a reactive response that may trigger old patterns of withdrawing or attacking. If you respond with criticism or defensiveness to your partner's revelations, you will damage your partner's trust in you and possibly endanger your new relationship.

Negotiating Differences

You and your partner have decided to stay together after the affair. You've discussed your fears and anxieties, and how the affair has affected you. You've just created an explicit agreement based on everything you desire concerning your relationship. This agreement will likely change over time, as you and your partner fine-tune it. During this dialogue, you and your partner have probably exposed some differences in how you want to move forward, and

I've provided the tools to discuss those differences. But what happens if you and your partner want different things, for instance, different levels of openness in your marriage? Is it still possible to save your marriage?

The answer is yes, as long as both of you are willing to work together on some of your more strongly held beliefs. If you want a polysexual relationship, where you can have sexual connections outside of the marriage, and your partner wants to remain in a totally closed relationship, a potential compromise might be to have a semi-open relationship, where you can share physical affection, but not sex, with people outside of the marriage. Another option might be to have your partner present and participating in any extramarital sexual experiences. But what if your partner absolutely refuses to consider any kind of openness at all? This is where you will need to talk it out using some of the dialogue techniques presented in this book, including validation, empathy, and "I" statements, to explore the worries and fears of each of you about the relationship.

The partner who wants more openness may fear that having a totally closed marriage might feel restrictive and dull, while the person who wants to keep the relationship closed might fear that opening up the marriage would mean losing her partner or that her partner no longer finds her attractive or interesting.

These are all valid concerns and need to be discussed openly and honestly to negotiate a relationship that works for both of you. The following are some questions to ask yourself if you find you are at an impasse and can't seem to agree on the level of openness in the relationship. You can use them as journaling exercises, questions to ask one another during a dialogue, or just talking points as you continue to explore your new agreement.

"What do I fear most about my partner's needs in this relationship?"

"Where am I willing to compromise my desires about the openness of our relationship?"

"Where am I not willing to compromise?"

"What's more important in this situation: that my partner agree on my way of doing things, or the integrity of my marriage?"

"If my partner doesn't come around to my way of thinking, would I consider leaving the relationship?"

"Is there a way to get my needs met even if my partner won't agree to what I want in the relationship?"

"How could I get those needs met?"

Time-Limited Compromises

One way to work around these sometimes-intractable problems is to agree to a time-limited trial period, in which the partner who doesn't want any openness agrees to as much openness as he can handle, but only for a limited time. For example, if one partner wants a closed marriage and the other wants polyamory, they may compromise by agreeing to have a semi-open relationship for three months, in which they can share physical affection with others but not sex, and can also agree on how much disclosure they want in the relationship. Do they want to share all of their experiences or none of them? The agreement might be that, unless one partner asks, the couple won't disclose any outside physical interactions. The point is to agree to a time-limited period in which the person who is the least comfortable with the other person's desire for openness can experiment with how it feels to have a low level of openness in the relationship. If that partner can handle this after the time period is up, the couple may agree to another time-limited trial period with a bit more openness and so on until the couple finds the perfect balance of safety and openness in their relation-ship. This process can take some time, and the couple must be able to address one another with openness, respect, and kindness throughout this exploratory process.

If, as a couple, you find that you can't negotiate without getting into bitter arguments or withdrawing into resentment, you may want to find an open-minded couples therapist who respects the validity of open relationships. This person may be able to help you compromise and negotiate a relationship that works for both of you.

One couple recently came to my office after agreeing to divorce, blaming cyber relationships for the demise of their marriage. They hoped that counseling would help them communicate as they split up and divided their assets. The primary reason they identified as the cause of their breakup was that he watched other couples have sex on the Internet.

This conflict was really about the implicit expectation that each partner had before they were married. She expected that any masturbation would stop once they got married and had a regular and frequent sex life. He assumed that he would still have his privacy and continue to experience his own erotic fantasies online, as long as they weren't with any "real" women.

In therapy they discussed what the future might hold if they were to stay together. A vision of a new monogamy for each of them was apparently very different. He couldn't see himself giving up online sex, and she couldn't understand why he wanted to continue. She took it personally, and he felt she was being too controlling.

One way they might work through this conflict, they decided, was to talk about what was actually turning him on in the online pornography and erotic sex shows that he was watching. She was curious about what he found so stimulating. He said he was excited by the thought of seeing another couple have sex, being voyeuristic. He wished they could do that in real life, together. He wanted to watch her, perhaps having sex with another man. She didn't think she would like it, but was willing to explore looking at these scenarios online with him. She wanted to try to be involved in the fantasy with her husband and to watch with him to see if it would be a turn-on for both of them. They talked more, and she said she could also explore some soft-core swapping if that was what he was into. By "soft core" she meant that she would not have intercourse with another man, and in fact anything below the waist would be off limits. But she might try a sexual encounter where her husband was present and could watch another man flirt with her, dance with her, and perhaps even touch her over her clothing. She said she would rather do this together and explore the fantasy with him than have him off on his own looking at it online. In fact, she admitted that she was slightly aroused at discussing the possibilities. It was the isolation that made her feel that she wanted to end the marriage, not necessarily his fantasy.

They put off the divorce and made a promise to explore this new aspect of their monogamy, at least temporarily.

Moving Forward with Your New Monogamy

Once you've made your agreement and formalized it by writing it down and possibly even holding a ceremony or ritualizing it in some way, it's time to live by your own new rules. Keep in mind that you will probably encounter some problems and delays in the beginning. One partner may get cold feet. One may feel insecure or shy.

Both of you may find that if your new monogamy includes opening your relationship, finding willing partners isn't easy. One may not find partners as quickly as the other, and resentments may build. It's almost guaranteed that one or both partners will feel jealous at some point. These are all normal reactions. It will be helpful, especially at first, to discuss these issues openly and frequently, possibly even every day. Use "I" statements or the Imago dialogue process outlined in this book as often as needed to make sure that both of you feel heard and valued.

If a particular aspect of the agreement continues to be a problem—for instance, if, despite having agreed to it, one partner just cannot feel comfortable with the other having sex outside the relationship—agree to table that item until you can renegotiate something that feels comfortable to both of you. It's not acceptable to keep doing things that are painful and rationalize this by saying "Well, you agreed to it." If a behavior is causing either of you pain, it must be stopped immediately until you can decide on a new agreement that works for both of you.

As you move forward and continue to reconnect and bond over your new experiences, both of you will probably warm up to the idea of having a completely honest and open connection to each other, and you may find that you become closer than ever. It matters less what your monogamy becomes and more how you feel and talk about it.

The following chapter discusses the next step in healing from infidelity: erotic recovery. This process will bring you and your partner closer in a physically intimate way, and help you heal from the sexual disconnection that may have been the root of the infidelity or caused by it.

CHAPTER 6

Erotic Recovery

Moving past an affair doesn't come easily to most people when infidelity causes erotic injury to your relationship. *Erotic injury* means that the partner who has been cheated on experiences an undermining of erotic confidence because of the infidelity. And the erotic intimacy between you has been damaged. Feelings of anger, rejection, and deep insecurity can emerge around your sexual relationship. It may be scary to think about reentering that intimate space right away. The erotic injury and the resulting hurt may take time to heal. Your fear may be that there is now such a great distance between you that it can never be repaired. This chapter will show you how to bridge that gap by helping you recover the erotic intimacy you have lost. This damaged intimate and erotic space has to be healed, because intimacy is necessary for rebuilding your relationship.

You may no longer feel attracted to your partner, or feel that your partner doesn't find you attractive. Attraction, sensuality, and sexuality are not just rooted in our genitals; they begin in our minds: in our emotions and in our feelings of trust. If you don't feel that you can trust your partner or your relationship, it's unlikely that you will feel interested in exploring an erotic connection right now.

Yet, if you are like many couples, an affair can trigger a new and intense sexual attraction to one another. Sometimes couples find they have more sex with one another right after an affair than they ever had in the past. Many couples are embarrassed to talk about this increase in sexual activity that happens immediately in the aftermath of infidelity. They don't want their partners to think it means that the affair is forgotten, or that it's an indication that their partners are forgiven. It doesn't mean that. Quite to the contrary, the affair is what makes the sex feel so intense now. The initial erotic injury creates a distance between the couple that can create a new attraction and longing for one another. The fear of losing each other can also trigger old feelings of sexual connection. And the need to be comforted in a time of real trauma can mean that you turn to one another in one of the only ways you may know how, in order to comfort each other in this very difficult time. And it may feel very intense and be the best sex you have ever had with each other. At the same time, it may be very confusing and emotionally frustrating. These mixed feelings can be disturbing at first, but they usually decrease over time.

However, not all couples experience this heightened eros right away after an affair. Cheating more often undermines the connection in the marriage or partnership, and can create a wall between you, blocking you from any desire for erotic intimacy. Erotic recovery, then, is a fundamental part of healing from the affair, because it addresses this very basic relationship need: to be erotically and intimately connected.

Erotic recovery encompasses all of the emotional, physical, and intimacy needs in your relationship, and means that you will need to do something about your basic sexual needs for trust, safety, and comfort. And you will also have to include risk and adventure in your relationship in order to create more passion in your erotic life. Until you and your partner can do these things and move beyond the erotic injury and repair your sex life together, the third party, the other man or woman, is still (metaphorically) in bed with you.

Moving from being emotionally and sexually disconnected after an affair to feeling erotically joined and ready to explore a new sexual life together may seem impossible, especially if you only recently discovered the affair and are still in intense pain. But if you have chosen to stay together for now—and given that you've read this far, this is a fair guess—working on your sex life is vital to your healing process.

The bridge between the two of you may seem too wide to cross at times. And yet you may find yourself wanting to reach out and hold your partner, and craving the feeling of being held in return. Sex can be a way to feel grounded, to feel warm, to remind both of you that there is still a reason to keep working on the relationship. Sexual intercourse can be a way to reenter each other in the most intimate physical way, but it also crosses an emotional boundary that goes beyond what can sometimes be expressed in words. Couples may find that what cannot be said out loud can instead be felt through tactile sensations on the skin.

And yet, this is why it can be so difficult to reconnect erotically. You may be able to come together, talk, and practice dialogue skills. You may even find yourselves becoming advanced at validating each other's feelings and yet still be unable to let yourself be vulnerable enough to touch each other intimately or make love in ways that you used to.

Most likely one of you will be more ready than the other to rebuild your sexual connection. If you are the partner that does not feel open to sex right now, you may feel pressure to do it anyway, either as a way to hold on to your spouse or prevent her from going back to the affair partner. This type of sexual hostage taking is not erotic recovery. It's normal to worry about being able to hold on to your partner after an affair. And it makes sense that you may wonder if your partner still finds you sexually attractive. You may worry that you aren't having sex often enough to keep your partner from cheating again, but if you are pressuring yourself to have sex with your partner because you are afraid of losing her, ask yourself if you truly have a desire to be closer to her. It's fine to push yourself past some discomfort and even to act as if you were comfortable until you find that you actually are. But using sex to manipulate your partner into staying won't, in the long run, give you the security you need. Your partner wants to be wanted, for herself—not because you are afraid. Ask yourself if you are making love out of fear or out of love for your partner. It's normal to feel some fear as well as love, but fear shouldn't be your total motivation.

If you find that you are using fear as a way to force yourself into bed with your partner, or if your partner is pressuring you for more intimacy than you're comfortable with, sit down with her first. Talk to your partner directly about your feelings. Share with her that you don't feel ready to have sex, and if you're open to doing some physical or intimate things short of sex, let her know what those things are. Tell her what you are ready for now. It helps to keep something in mind that you are ready to do. This might sound like "Right now, I'm still nervous about having sex, but I do want to _____." Sex doesn't have to be the goal of erotic recovery right away. Erotic connection can mean taking your time and connecting in other ways first, using intimate physical time as a way to move toward sexual intercourse.

A Change from "Goal-Oriented" Sex

Many times the focus of sex is on getting to the "finish line," or achieving orgasm. Sometimes when a couple takes away the goal of getting to the end zone, the process becomes more enjoyable and less stressful. The benefit of being focused on the moment, not the end result, is that it creates less stress for both partners and less anxiety about performance. Having fewer stress-related sexual-performance issues means a decrease in sexual dysfunction and anxiety.

Approaching sex in a less "goal-oriented" (that is, "orgasm-oriented") approach can be a whole new way of experiencing sex for both men and women. For couples recovering from an affair, it can be a way to slow down the process and relearn what sex and sensuality are really about.

You may be wondering *Am I still attractive to my partner? Do I still have what it takes to be in a sexual relationship?* and other questions that come up normally around sexual self-esteem. After your partner cheats, it may take time to recover your own power in bed and to feel sexy and confident again. One way to do that is to find a way to slow down the process and reconnect to each other without the pressure of performance.

A couple working toward a healthier and more connected sex life after infidelity can benefit from an exercise that removes the routine of sex from the traditional pattern: kissing, foreplay, intercourse, orgasm, snuggling, and sleep. Slowing down the process by focusing on being in the moment with the total experience of love-making, and working together to make it feel positive and healthy can help both partners feel more comfortable and trusting. This increases intimacy, especially after the ambivalence and insecurity resulting from an affair.

This chapter presents a step-by-step plan for you and your partner to use in your erotic recovery process. The erotic date night will help you get closer to one another in a slower, more proscribed way that is flexible enough to allow you and your partner to explore intimacy at your own pace, without orgasm or even intercourse as the main goal.

Later, an even more detailed process will be described for those of you who want a more structured approach. Use these tools as you feel comfortable adding them into your erotic recovery, and feel free to adjust them to fit your situation and emotional states.

Later in the chapter, the fantasy spectrum is discussed as a way to understand and talk about the sexual wishes and fantasies of both of you. Sharing fantasies and expressing curiosity about sexuality can be a fun and exciting way to renew your sexual connection in the aftermath of erotic injury, but it also serves as an ongoing tool of connection long after the erotic recovery process is completed.

Your Erotic Date

Even if you aren't ready to have sex with your partner yet, committing to erotic recovery can still begin anytime. One way to commit to the erotic recovery process without focusing on whether or not you are going to have intercourse any time soon is to commit to a weekly erotic date.

The step-by-step process for erotic recovery presented later in this chapter asks that you not have intercourse at all for the first few dates, to give both partners time and space to get used to physically reconnecting with one another. Intercourse is not the definition of eroticism. Racing to the finish line of ejaculation or climax is not the ultimate goal. Being together in ways that focus on bringing each other pleasure, and being generous and sexually empathetic is more erotic than focusing on who climaxes when.

An *erotic date* is a special time that you set aside to focus on this special aspect of your relationship, and it takes up only a few hours per week. The important part of making a date for sexual and erotic activity is that it sets aside sacred space and time dedicated to your relationship. The rest of your hours together during the week can be set aside for your companionship and working on the rest of the relationship issues that you are moving through. But your erotic date time is necessary if you are to move forward in your new monogamy. If you don't dedicate these few hours a week to your sexual relationship, then you may find that you move farther apart instead of closer together.

That said, never let yourself feel forced into sex or any erotic behavior that doesn't feel comfortable for you. Sexual coercion is never acceptable, even when it comes from a spouse or an intimate partner. Similarly, don't manipulate your partner with your sexual needs and do not use sex as the only way to get your emotional needs met at this time. When you choose a time for your erotic date, plan it for once a week and on the same day and time every week. Choose a day or evening when you both have time to relax and when you can make focusing on your partner your priority. If you have children, consider arranging for a babysitter, or have them spend time with relatives or at a friend's house. You may feel resistant to this idea at first, but I encourage you to try creating your date night to allow yourselves total freedom to relax together. If you are committed to rebuilding your relationship, you will need this time alone, if you can make it happen.

Initially you might feel that planning sex means that your love life is no longer spontaneous, that it's no longer romantic or genuine. Yet making a date with your partner for eros actually allows for more romance and authenticity. After all, when you were first dating, you probably had to make plans when you wanted to be together. Think of planning a sex date today the way you did when you were first dating. It's a way to look forward to being together, to discovering each other all over again.

These dates can be an important part of creating spontaneity and special time in your relationship. It shows commitment and intention, and adds a caring and erotic element. And, ironically, you can be as spontaneous as you want—if you plan it.

As you begin to plan your date, notice that you or your partner may feel some resistance that might take the form of excuses like "We'll be tired then" or "We won't have time." This may actually be fear that is surfacing about intimacy. You might be afraid that you won't want to be with your partner or that when the night arrives, he won't want to be with you. Recognize that this resistance is normal and that you should have your date anyway. Part of the reason for the erotic date process is to reconnect in a way that shows each of you that you are wanted sexually by one another, and that you can move past feeling erotically disconnected.

Anticipation

One of the reasons your date should be at the same time every week is so that you begin to anticipate having erotic time, even before your date night rolls around.

You may find that you begin thinking about what will happen several days before the date night arrives. This is what I call *erotic anticipation*. Even if you haven't had sex in many years, as you start to reintegrate sensual and erotic experience into your lives on a regular basis, the "practice" of an erotic date will train your body, mind, and spirit to expect sensuality and intimacy and to anticipate them.

If you can move through the initial discomfort or awkwardness, you will find that eventually, you will both look forward to this sacred time together, when you can explore your erotic connection and regain your sexual confidence.

Some couples continue date nights for years. Try to commit to, at least, a three-month plan of erotic dates once a week. At the end of that three-month period, look back and see how you did as a couple. Did you meet every week? Did you show up late? Did you take it seriously? Did you have fun? Talk about how your erotic dates improved your relationship. Continuing them is in your best interest as a couple, so you may want to sign up for another three months. Continue for as long as you can, and erotic dates will become an integral part of your love life and your erotic vision going forward.

Sex as a Practice

A good sex life is a practice, just like yoga or meditation, or even playing the piano. Engaging erotically with each other on a regular basis means you are committing to the practice of an intimate relationship. The more you invest in this practice, the greater the benefit.

Your erotic date is not a "going out" night. It's different from movie night or dancing night. Avoid heavy meals or too much alcohol. Eating dinner out or drinking too much wine is not likely to make you want to come home and make love; it will most likely just make you want to come home and sleep.

Resistance

If one or both of you don't feel ready to reconnect erotically, your resistance to the idea is perfectly normal. At certain times in your relationship, you may even feel repulsed by your partner, as your resentment and fear surface from time to time. This is a natural way that your psyche protects itself from intimacy. You don't want to become vulnerable to getting hurt again.

There may be times when your partner wants to make love and you don't. You might be afraid, angry, or shut down, and sometimes a "just do it" mentality doesn't work. If you are willing to continue the schedule of showing up for your date night no matter how you feel, many of your feelings may change over time. They may improve or even become more difficult. If you are feeling extremely resistant to intimacy with your partner, set some limits on the night.

Limits

Setting limits can include statements like "I am willing to be in bed with you, but not to make love" or "I am willing to be naked, but please don't touch me until I touch you first; I may need time to feel comfortable." Share with your partner any ways that would help you feel more relaxed.

Janet, a forty-year-old housewife who had been married to Paul for twelve years, had trouble with their date nights for several months, but kept it up. She told him how difficult it was for her. During the week she could ignore her feelings, but on weekends when they would meet in the bedroom for their erotic date nights, it became a very emotional experience for her: "I really needed Paul to let me know every date night that he was totally there for me. He had spent so much time with his affair partner, wining and dining her and taking her to expensive hotels, that every time we tried to meet for our erotic date night, I remembered what he did for her and I felt cheated. I wanted to know that he was going to make as much effort for me. It wasn't enough that he just walked up the stairs to our bedroom and took off his clothes.

"I told him how I felt, and he made some changes. He would go up first, light candles, put clean sheets on the bed, and put some music on. He made an effort. But it was still hard for me at first; I cried for the first hour every time. He just held me. After a while, when he didn't quit, and kept showing up and lighting the candles, I knew he really wanted to be there. One night I came home and found a dozen roses on the bedside table. I really felt that we had turned a corner somehow. Although it's still hard, and one bouquet isn't going to fix it, it's easier now, and I look forward to it. I keep tissues handy, though. I still cry."

An erotic date is dedicated time carved out of your week where you simply close your bedroom door, turn off the TV, and set up the room as a sacred, erotic space to practice erotic recovery together. This may mean lighting a candle, turning on music, or just holding each other. Or it could mean taking a bath together and sleeping naked. Or it may mean a specific and guided practice of exercises like the ones later in this chapter.

When date night arrives, know that you will have some type of intimate contact, even if you don't feel like it in the moment. Sometimes beginning contact with each other can create arousal or even just an emotional and physical closeness that sparks a new experience for the two of you. Exploring what feels right can begin within the context of the sex date.

Preparing for Your Date

Leading up to the date, make sure you put effort into preparing for your special time together. And remember, it doesn't matter who initiates the date night or who reminds the other that it's time. If your partner forgets, it doesn't mean that she loves you less or that you want it more. Just continue the pattern of once-a-week dates. The routine may change over time.

Resistance is normal, and your relationship issues may be triggered. Conflict will arise during this process, as in everything else you maneuver and negotiate in your lives together. Try to let arguing or power struggles be off limits during date night.

Starting about four days prior to the erotic date, begin the buildup to the night by using small acts to help create anticipation for the time you will spend together. Show your partner physical affection several times during the week leading up to the erotic date. Attempt to connect by whispering in your partner's ear the things you are looking forward to on your erotic date night. Bring home a surprise that you may use on the date. This might be a card or small token gift. Or the surprise might be something you can use for sex if you are planning a more erotic date, for instance, a bottle of massage oil or lube.

If you have an intention that you want to set before each date night, speak it out loud. Do you want to ensure that both of you feel loved and desired? Do you want to remind yourselves of the fun date nights you used to have when you were first dating? Do you want to feel sexy again? Make sure that you tell your partner your implicit expectations so that there are no misunderstandings. And ask your partner what her expectations are. You will have a better chance of meeting each other's needs if you can share what you are wishing for before the night begins.

Date Night

On the day of the date, try to create an atmosphere in the room that will remind both of you that this is a sacred, erotic space for you to play in together. Light candles, put out fresh flowers, and put soft sheets on the bed. Pick out music that both of you might enjoy.

Be sure to think about what you need to make you happy in your surroundings. Do you like warm air on your skin, a light scent in the air, or soft or fast music? Think about how you can make this an erotic and sensual experience for yourself. Is there something special you want to wear because it makes you feel sexy? Try not to only think about how to please your partner; think about pleasing yourself as well. You are creating an environment where desire can flourish, once it is aroused.

When it's time for the date, keep your expectations open and reasonable. If the evening goes as you envisioned it, then great. Process it together by telling your partner that night and the next day what you appreciated about it. Leave your partner a note in the morning or even in his lunch box or briefcase. Or send your partner a text message that says what you liked about the date.

Arousal and Desire

For women, arousal often comes before desire. Don't wait for the desire to hit. You may not feel desire first. Once you are physically aroused and turned on, you may then feel some desire, but even then your feelings can be confusing. Don't let the feelings in your body decide for you either way. Your arousal or lack thereof can make you feel betrayed by your own sexuality. You may be upset that you feel nothing when you really want to, or you may feel the opposite: *How come I feel so turned on by my spouse after what he did to me?* Don't be angry with yourself for either reaction. Your body is responding in the way that it needs to in the moment.

As you are ready for more sensual contact, your erotic date can be a place to explore more intimate and sexual touch and play. You'll know when you are ready, when the two of you start to naturally explore things you can do together. One of you may feel hesitant and less ready than the other. Go slowly and take your time. There are many ways to experience sensual connection, including lying naked together, using soft touch, massaging each other, touching your partner in a sensual way, rubbing your hands lightly over your own body while your partner watches, or sharing fantasies.

Exercise 6.1 Dialogue for Erotic Date Night

This exercise, which can be perfect for your erotic date night, uses the Imago dialogue introduced in chapter 2 to help you share some of the things you would like to try together in bed, even if you choose not to do so that night.

1. Make some time during an erotic date night to share one thing that you are already doing on your erotic date nights that you like and would like more of.

2. Take turns sharing and mirroring back to each other what you hear.

3. Then share with one another something new you would like to try, and simply mirror back to each other what you hear. Talking about

fantasies can be a real turn-on, so don't rush to bring anything into action right away.

4. Just validate for your partner what you can. Does it make sense that this would be a turn-on for him? If not, ask him more about what is exciting about this particular fantasy.

5. If you start to get triggered by memories of the affair or begin to feel hurt or upset, slow down and ask for what you need. Do you need a hug or for your partner to hold you? Do you need appreciation? Ask your partner to tell you three things he appreciates about you, and share three things you appreciate about him. Appreciation has a way of reconnecting you whenever you start to feel a disconnect between you. It may be possible to go back to sharing fantasies and turn-ons at that point. This can lead to an important night of sharing sensual pleasure.

6. If the date doesn't live up to your expectations, which is likely to happen on many occasions in the beginning (remember, this is a practice, and it takes time to get good at it), try to reframe the experience for yourself by reminding each other that if you actually showed up for each other, the night was a success. If you felt at all connected to your partner, it was a success. If you practiced a new intimacy skill or even revisited a tried-and-true one, then the date was a step in the direction of a new life together.

If you haven't had sex yet or don't feel ready for real intimate contact, the next six-week assignment is a good way to start. In this assignment, you will work up to being more sexual during your intimate contact. It can take the entire six weeks to be comfortable with each other and ready for intercourse.

Exercise 6.2   Six Weeks of Great Erotic Dates

Connection that refocuses both partners on sensuality and physical intimacy can help change the dynamic and the relationship for the better. If you are having trouble connecting sexually, or want to reconnect slowly and carefully, use this six-week protocol and take it seriously. Read this exercise in its entirety first. Adapted from the Masters and Johnson sensate focus exercise (Masters, Johnson, and Kolodny 1986), this exercise reworks their concepts and includes my own erotic recovery concepts. The exercise will slow down the erotic reconnection process and integrate your new monogamy into your affair recovery.

This exercise will take place over six weeks, but you can extend it and slow it down as well, perhaps making each night a two-week exercise. This is the first exercise that you will practice on erotic date night, when you have uninterrupted time to practice erotic recovery. Later you can use erotic date night to practice other erotic expansion activities.

Establish the weekly day and time of your erotic date. Integrate the idea into your schedule. Begin to practice intimate connection weekly. These six weeks can be intimate even if they aren't sexual.

Before each date night, decide who will be the sender and who will be the receiver. You will each have a turn, so choose who will be the sender first on the first week. You might decide to switch off going first and take turns on different nights, or you can both send and receive in one night.

For this six-week period, you will consciously avoid intercourse for three weeks prior to your first instance of sexual intercourse. By that time your erotic date will have been firmly established in your schedule. Focus on activities on erotic date night that promote eye contact, sensuality, and each other's pleasure through both giving and receiving.

Anxiety, anger, sadness, grief, or a need to prove yourself may often come up during sex. At times one or both of you may hide under the covers, keep the lights off and clothes on, or even fight off any touch. Other times you may find yourself crying before, during, and after touch. These are all normal reactions, and unless you are hurting yourself or your partner, make space for all of your feelings and have some tissues handy if you need them to wipe your eyes.

This exercise allows time and space for you to focus on the idea of pleasure and to slow down the process and take the focus off sexual performance.

Night one. The goal of night one is to massage each other without touching the "bikini" areas. This means that you will touch each other in any way that feels good. But you will avoid focusing on the genitals and avoid orgasm as the goal. In fact, orgasm and intercourse are off limits on night one.

For some couples, achieving orgasm can be a challenge, even more so ever since the affair. It's okay to take orgasm off the table as an option throughout the entire six-week exercise. The less pressure you each feel to achieve anything, the more relaxed the experience will be for both of you.

The receiver lies on a soft bed or a blanket on the floor, and the sender massages and explores the receiver's body. Use massage oil that is perfume free to avoid irritation. The sender should start at the extremities and move inward, or start at the head and move down to the feet. The sender should work in a sensual manner, in a way that she thinks her partner will appreciate.

The sender starts on the back of the receiving partner, with firm strokes going from slow to fast, or soft to hard. The receiving partner works on breathing and receiving, noticing what feelings surface. Is there resistance, anger, frustration? Is there sadness, love, longing?

Just notice the feelings, without trying to change them. Let the feelings come through and don't judge or hold on to a desire to accomplish anything.

If you are the receiver, you may notice that there are frozen or resistant parts of your body as you feel the massage strokes, or you may not feel anything at all. Perhaps you are numb. You may either resent the strokes or welcome them. Experience and welcome all the feelings without judgment.

You may be surprised at how being restricted from touching the "bikini" area takes the pressure off you and your partner, and allows you to explore each other's bodies in a way that's simply pleasurable and purely sensual, with no other goal. Revisit the landscape of each other's bodies, remembering that this is a very generous experience, both the giving and taking. If you are the sender, concentrate on the feel of your partner's skin, and if you are the receiver, try to focus on the feel of your partner's hands. Remember, the only goal is to be as much in the moment as possible.

Whenever you decide, the receiver can offer feedback, but only on a 1-to-5 feedback scale in which 1 means uncomfortable or almost painful, and the sender will know to move away from that stroke or touch; 2 is somewhat uncomfortable but by no means unpleasant; 3 is very nice but more neutral; 4 is very good and feels wonderful; and 5 means intense pleasure and the desire for continued touch. The sender should ask "How does that feel?" or "How is that?" The receiver should respond by sticking only to the 1-to-5 scale.

In this exercise we refrain from using words to avoid sounding judgmental, critical, or demanding. This can also help get rid of embarrassment or shame about asking for what you want. Let the 1-to-5 scale describe the experience of sensation reception, and try not to use any descriptive words.

The use of numbers instead of words will allow you to fully experience the sensations without the added complication of emotional response. If you are the receiver, this can help you simply experience the strokes without shifting too thoroughly into the part of your brain that controls language. In other words, you don't have to think too much before responding. No words or explanations are necessary. Only receiving and feeling the sensations, and communicating those feelings are needed.

The sender should focus only on sending the sensation of the massage stroke. Trying to get the receiver to experience a rating of 4 or 5 is desirable but not necessary. If you are the sender, notice your feelings. Is there resentment, guilt, wonder? What's going on inside as you hear your partner's feedback about the massage? Can you change the strokes so that they feel better to your partner? Just notice your thoughts about your partner's reaction. Are you surprised that your partner is reacting to the strokes this way? Would you have thought otherwise? Without judging your performance or your partner's receptivity, take it in as information and continue your movements, noticing how the stroking feels to you as you listen to the music, if you've chosen to play music—and breathe.

Breath is an important part of this exercise. If, as the sender, you can time your breathing to go in and out with the movement of your hands, this will give you more power and awareness during the massage, and with your partner. You may feel a deeper and more intense connection with the receiver as you massage him if you are connected to your own breath.

And if you can connect to the rhythm of the recipient's breath as you are inhaling and exhaling, you may feel a unique circular rhythm to the experience that you might not have noticed before. You may notice that you feel some of your partner's emotions as you massage him, or you may feel some sexual or erotic feelings. Just breathe, notice these feelings, and try not to judge or act on them at this time.

The receptive partner now turns over onto his back, and the same thing continues. There is no breast or genital touching at this time.

For the receiver, it can be very powerful to hold in your mind some appreciative and positive thoughts and feelings about your partner as she touches you. Imagine your partner surrounded by white light, and send positive and kind thoughts about her while her energy is going into yours. This is a way to clear the energy between you, even if only temporarily.

The exercise ends with the sender slowing down her strokes and deepening her breathing. The sender slowly lies on top of the receiver with her full body, and both partners breathe deeply with closed eyes to seal the experience. Breathe for at least three minutes or ten deep breaths. Holding your partner's hands palm to palm as you do this can seal your energies more completely. Taking a last deep breath, the sender moves off the receiver, and you may switch places or move into sleep.

Note that no overt sexual interaction takes place during this activity, and yet you may both feel aroused or desire something more erotic. Hold on to that desire and sit with it. Honor the idea that tonight doesn't have to be the night that you act on those urges.

Night two. Follow the same directions as for night one, but now add in the breasts and genitals, with the same amount of attention and direction as the rest of the body. After a while the receiver can use the 1-to-5 feedback scale, but the goal here is *not* orgasm or penetration.

Night three. The same directions apply: massage, including breast and genital touch, and verbal feedback on a scale from 1 to 5, but now you can apply extra focus to the genitals and breasts, or whatever parts of the receiver's body are the most responsive to the sender's touch. This time, the 1-to-5 reporting is optional, but words are still off limits. If you don't want to use the 1-to-5 scale, you can use moans, groans, and other sounds to indicate enjoyment. The goal is to stop right before orgasm.

Ironically, with the prohibition against orgasm, many couples find that they want to move into an orgasmic connection. Sometimes when something is "forbidden," it becomes even more enticing. If you are both feeling responsive, you may want to modify this experience for night three. But let yourselves hold off on penetration; remember that anticipation creates a more exciting erotic experience and increases the longing and attraction between you.

Night four. Now you can repeat all of the previous steps, and if both partners desire it, you can add orgasm, but without penetration of any kind. Only nonpenetrative orgasm and manipulation are permitted tonight. It's important that, for heterosexual couples, the woman always orgasm first, so if you are adding orgasm to night four, she should have her orgasm prior to the male orgasm. This assures that her needs are addressed before the man's refractory period, or the time after the male orgasm when he will need to rest to restore his energy and testosterone level in order to achieve another erection.

Night five. If desired, you can add penetration to this sensual and erotic experience. But the night must start with giving and receiving massage. First, decide who will be the receiver and who will be the sender. Take note of any emotions that you feel.

Night six. Penetration is the goal here. Make the moment of penetration as sensual an experience as possible. Work up to it slowly. Start with massage, concentrating on receiving and giving. Add in orgasm if you feel open to the possibility. Now, in addition, you'll add another element: emotional disclosure.

Talk about any feelings that come up at any time during the night. Check in with one another, asking questions such as "How are you feeling now?" If at any point, either of you has an emotion that creates withdrawal or shutdown, you can call a time-out and start over. Starting over doesn't mean that the night ends, just that you return to the massage portion of the night until your emotions calm down or change to allow for orgasm.

Talk about your feelings before, during, and after intercourse, if you decide to have full penetration. Don't attempt to intellectualize your partner's feelings or try to get him out of his emotional state. Avoid saying things like "You shouldn't feel that way" or "Don't cry." Only make validating and empathizing statements; for example, "It sounds as if you are feeling _____" or "It makes sense that you are feeling _____" and "Do you need a break?" And if your partner says yes, then go back to the massage until he is ready to move to genital massage, penetration (if you choose), and orgasm.

After the evening of sexual connection and pleasure, share with your partner what you appreciated about the night. You might say "One thing I really appreciated about this night was _____," and then switch and receive one appreciation from your partner. See if each of you can share three things you appreciate about the night and each other.

This is a six-week exercise, or it can be a twelve-week exercise. Or you may want to use this exercise over many months or a year, to establish a deep and connecting base of trust that brings your bodies and hearts into alignment.

On the other hand, you may be like some couples that last about two weeks and are ready to move into a full erotic life together, sharing their deepest sexual fantasies. Even if you are one of those couples who are taking things slowly, try to wait the six weeks and follow the protocol. It can take time to build trust and establish a new intimate connection. Even breaking old patterns can take several weeks or months. This six-week period is the time you may need to heal. Imagine that you have had a deep injury and that you both need time to recover. Give yourselves the time that you need.

Attraction and Longing Happen in the Space between You

After an affair, it can be a painful revelation that your partner had sexual experiences and desires that didn't include you. However, this may also increase or create a new type of curiosity. What is this newfound sexuality in your partner? Can you become curious about that? Many couples find that this new curiosity can create a new longing and attraction.

How do you move from that new longing to a new erotic life together that is filled with an open dialogue and new fantasies?

The Fantasy Spectrum

Erotic curiosity is any energy that contains thoughts, fantasies, and desires of a sexual or erotic nature. All warm-blooded creatures have sex. But what separates us from other mammals is our capacity to *eroticize* sex. We do this by using our minds to have sex, as well as our bodies. We all have thoughts about erotic things. We use our imaginations to create erotic scenes and fantasies. We then use these fantasies as energy to fuel our passion.

We become erotically curious about each other in the beginning of a relationship, when we are learning about one another and longing for connection. This curiosity can lead to fantasy and ultimately to erotic action.

In long-term relationships, erotic curiosity can decrease over time. You assume you know what your partner desires. You decide that you know what your partner doesn't want. When you close off your curiosity, your natural wondering about what your partner might like decreases. This may affect your longing and attraction as you imagine that your partner isn't interested in expanding. This may not be true at all. Perhaps you have only stopped imagining the possibility.

Most of us have a natural need to grow in our erotic lives. Given free rein and an encouraging partner, imagination really has no bounds. That doesn't mean you have to act on any of the things you fantasize about.

Your erotic imagination includes three things: curiosity, fantasy, and erotic action. This is the spectrum of normal erotic thought. This illustrates how your fantasy life plays out in your mind and in your life.

The *fantasy spectrum* is a way to think of your thoughts, fantasies, and desires as being on a continuum, from simple thoughts about sexual acts to full-blown erotic fantasies.

Another area to consider on the spectrum is power. Power indicates two things: whether you are submissive or dominant, and whether or not you are more receptive or directive.

There's no right or wrong place to be, but by deciding where you and your partner fall on the spectrum, you can explore fantasies, thoughts, and actions that may help as you journey into your new erotic life and your new monogamy agreement.

Anything on your own fantasy spectrum is normal for you. At one end of the spectrum are erotic thoughts: things you are *curious* about. You might think about certain things, including specific sex acts, erotic games, and sexy clothes, or you may even have thoughts about other people. But being curious doesn't mean you necessarily want to do something about it.

Being erotically curious about something or someone doesn't necessarily mean you fantasize about these things; they are sometimes just passing thoughts. Maybe you have read about a sex act or seen something in a movie that intrigues you, but you don't think much about it or give it much energy. Still, there is curiosity and wondering.

The things you are curious about and fantasize about are on the middle of the spectrum. Fantasies are thoughts and pictures in your mind, perhaps of people or scenarios that turn you on. Maybe you share these things with your partner, letting her in on your fantasy life. And many times you may keep your fantasies secret. These fantasies may come to mind when you masturbate or when you have sex with your partner, but you don't necessarily talk about them.

What you think about in the privacy of your mind is your own personal, fantastic movie theater on the inner screen of your imagination. What you *do* about your thoughts and fantasies are your erotic actions. Acting out a fantasy or curiosity can be great, or it can be hurtful for you or others. Actions can be healthy or unhealthy, depending on your relationship and how they affect your partner.

Or, sometimes you find enough security in your relationship to talk to your partner about your fantasies, but you don't act them out. They stay on a fantasy level only and can serve as erotic energy or fuel for your sexual relationship.

At the opposite end of the spectrum are the erotic fantasies you want to take into reality and make happen. You have a fantasy and, somehow, with your partner, make it a reality. Sometimes you need a catalyst to have your fantasies come to fruition. That catalyst can be anything that pushes you from curiosity to fantasy to *action*.

When you do share your fantasies with your partner, it's important to clarify with your partner which of those fantasies you actually want to act on. Perhaps you like the thought of something and it turns you on to think about doing it with your partner, but you aren't sure you ever really want to act it out.

You may have a fantasy about doing something with someone other than your partner, and never choose to share this with your partner. Or, given your new monogamy agreement, you might. You may have a fantasy about an act that could never actually happen but, by exploring it with your partner, find elements or dynamics within the fantasy that you could integrate into your sex life. This is an important way to conceptualize your fantasy world. If you have things you want to share with your partner about your desires and longings, it helps to be able to identify those desires.

Some people know what their fantasies are. Sometimes they are unsure of what to ask for, because they can't identify what they long for. Look at the following "Fantasy Spectrum" and try to identity where your fantasies lie: on the dominant or submissive side of the spectrum, receptive or directive, just curious or wanting to act on a sexual thought.

Fantasy Spectrum

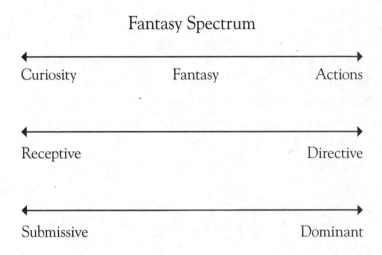

| Curiosity | Fantasy | Actions |

| Receptive | | Directive |

| Submissive | | Dominant |

Exercise 6.3   Erotic Curiosity

One way to share your fantasies is to begin to explore the things you are merely curious about. Maybe you don't even know yet what those things are.

The following is a list for both of you to explore your fantasies and see what you are curious about. Take some time separately to go through this list and notice what piques your curiosity. Some things on this list may be a turnoff and some a turn-on. Rate them on a scale from 1 to 5, in which 1 means you don't feel turned on when you think of this erotic fantasy and 5 means you are totally turned on just from reading about it. A rating of 2, 3, or 4 falls somewhere in between for you.

You can write your answers on a separate piece of paper or in your journal, and then find a time to discuss them with your partner. This review can be an exciting conversation about your curiosities and even your fantasies. Take time to sit down together and go over your lists. You can trade lists that you have marked up with your answers or discuss them out loud. Remember, this is not about promising to act out each other's fantasies. Do your best to empathize with each other.

This exercise is, first, a way to recognize your own erotic curiosities and, second, a way to see which of them actually *are* fantasies. Third, by discussing your answers together, you can find out what it feels like to share your erotic curiosities and fantasies by communicating openly with your partner. Finally, you may discover things you eventually want to act on.

On a scale from 1 to 5, how curious are you about the following activities?

I am curious about new ways of experiencing sexual pleasure. _____

I am curious about ways of pleasuring my partner. _____

I am curious about ways other people experience sexual satisfaction. _____

I am curious about sexual acts I may never have experienced. _____

I am curious about my partner's sexual fantasies. _____

I am curious about exploring my own sexual fantasies. _____

I am curious about receiving oral sex. _____

I am curious about performing oral sex on my partner. _____

I am curious about different sexual positions. _____

I am curious about how to have an orgasm. _____

I am curious about how to give my partner an orgasm. _____

I am curious about how to talk out loud to my partner during sex. _____

I am curious about what it would be like to have my partner talk during sex. _____

I am curious about sharing my fantasies with my partner. _____

I am curious about reading erotica. _____

I am curious about the G-spot. _____

I am curious about extending my orgasm. _____

I am curious about extending my partner's orgasm. _____

I am curious about having multiple orgasms. _____

I am curious about giving multiple orgasms. _____

I am curious about what stimulates me. _____

I am curious about how to ask for my erotic needs to be met. _____

I am curious about how to talk to my partner about what my partner desires during sex. _____

I am curious about pornography. _____

I am curious about dominance and submission. _____

I am curious about sadism and masochism. _____

I am curious about bondage. _____

I am curious about having sex with someone of the same gender. _____

I am curious about watching my partner have sex with someone else. _____

I am curious about having my partner watch me have sex with someone else. _____

I am curious about having sex with more than one person at a time. _____

I am curious about having sex with many people at the same time. _____

I am curious about my partner watching me have sex with several people at the same time. _____

I am curious about watching my partner have sex with several people. _____

I am curious about spanking. _____

I am curious about sex toys. _____

I am curious about vibrators. _____

I am curious about lubricants. _____

I am curious about anal sex. _____

I am curious about wearing leather. _____

I am curious about being tied up. _____

I am curious about using food as a sex object. _____

I am curious about having my hair pulled during sex. _____

I am curious about what other people of my same sex fantasize about. _____

I am curious about what my partner fantasizes about. _____

I am curious about something that is not on this list. _____

If this list brings up thoughts and fantasies for you, write down one fantasy that you want to act out.

_____

Erotic Curiosity vs. Action

The higher the level of curiosity, the more likely you or your partner will have a fantasy about that erotic thought. In other words, some things you are curious about may eventually be something you fantasize about, but the more curious you are, the more likely you'll fantasize about that act. But not all fantasies lead to action.

Sometimes a fantasy has just as much "energy" or "fuel" for the relationship as actually acting something out. Simply having a dialogue with your partner about a fantasy can raise the heat and passion between you. Once a fantasy is out in the open, it can become something you talk about often, or just use on special occasions to spice up your sex life.

If you are clear with your partner that you have a fantasy you would like to share but aren't ready to act out, then it can be easier to share it. For example, you might be more likely to share your fantasy of being suspended during sex if you aren't worried that your partner will run out to the hardware store immediately and buy hooks for the ceiling!

Submissive vs. Dominant

Also on the fantasy spectrum are two general categories: submissive and dominant. Our thoughts and fantasies tend to reveal a preference to be submissive or controlled in bed, or to be more dominant and controlling. Being erotically under someone else's control falls on the submissive side of the spectrum. Or you might have thoughts and fantasies about being more dominant, and like the thought of being in erotic control of your partner. Some people like to be dominant in bed but don't like the thought of being too controlling; it makes them feel awkward to be too bossy. One way of being dominant but not too controlling might mean simply giving direction or leading the way, but not actually controlling all the moves in bed. Being submissive may mean being open and welcoming in sensation and experience. Having this ability to receive can be just as powerful as being the one in charge. Both of these categories function as their own fantasy spectrum, with many variations of control, and the erotic power plays can be acted out in many ways.

Fantasy Spectrum

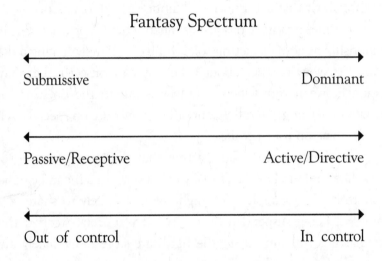

Submissive   Dominant

Passive/Receptive   Active/Directive

Out of control   In control

Notice whether you have a tendency to have fantasies on the "submissive" side and enjoy being out of control sometimes. Your fantasies on the "Fantasy Spectrum" will be more about being sexually controlled, or submissive. Sexual submissives might enjoy thoughts of being tied up, or being "forced" to have sex or to act in other "forbidden" ways. (Being "forced" in this instance is about acing out a submissive fantasy.)

Knowing this about yourself can give you valuable insight into your own sexuality and sexual needs. It can also help you move forward in your new erotic relationship with your partner as you describe your erotic needs and desires. Identifying yourself and showing your partner "This is where I am" on the spectrum can give your partner a clear vision of who you are erotically and your real desires.

If you are more dominant and enjoy thoughts of being in control sexually, you may have fantasies such as being on top during missionary sex, blindfolding your partner, or ordering your partner to perform oral sex.

It's normal to enjoy both: being submissive sometimes and being dominant at other times. Most people have the capacity to enjoy each experience to some extent. Yet by reading this chapter, you might find that your fantasy life has a tendency to fall on one side or the other.

Exercise 6.4 What Are Your Fantasies?

In this exercise, notice which fantasies are exciting to you. What fantasies turn you on as you think of them, and what fantasies would you like to act out?

The following is a list of common fantasies that fall on both ends of the submissive-dominant spectrum. They include a wide range of erotic interests. Go through the list and see what turns you on. Notice what gives you sexual energy and what is intriguing. Perhaps none of these fantasies is sexy for you. Write down your own fantasies and add anything that feels erotic. Note what you are curious about, what you have a fantasy about, and what you actually would like to take into action.

You can do this alone or with your partner. I recommend trying it alone first and then sharing your list with your partner, using some of the communication techniques you have learned so far. By first marking each fantasy with a number that indicates your interest level, you will have a clear way to share with your partner your level of erotic curiosity.

Mark each item using a scale from 1 to 5 in which 1 means you have some curiosity about this fantasy and are somewhat turned on by it; 2 means you have or could have fantasies about this and it turns you on, but you aren't sure you want to actually do it; 3 means you may want to act out this fantasy; 4 means you definitely would like this fantasy to come true; and 5 means you would like to start planning this fantasy right away. If you feel neutral about the fantasy, leave it blank.

Fantasies:

Rose petals on the bed   _____

Making love outdoors   _____

Taking pictures of each other naked   _____

Dancing naked together   _____

Doing a strip tease for your partner   _____

Having sex in the shower   _____

Having sex in other rooms of the house   _____

Submissive Fantasies:

Watching two people have sex   _____

Being seduced   _____

Watching your partner masturbate   _____

Masturbating in front of your partner   _____

Being dominated   _____

Receiving oral sex   _____

Being spanked   _____

Being tied up   _____

Wearing a collar   _____

Having your hair pulled _____

Submitting to an order and thanking your partner _____

Being caned or whipped _____

Having your toes sucked _____

Having sex outdoors or in public places _____

Domination Fantasies:

Dressing up in leather _____

Role-playing with costumes (for example, stripper, cowboy, doctor) _____

Wearing boots or high heels _____

Tying up your partner _____

Putting handcuffs on your partner _____

Putting a collar on your partner _____

Pinching your partner _____

Using a cane, riding crop, or whip to threaten _____

Using a cane, riding crop, or whip to inflict sensation _____

Blindfolding your partner _____

Having your partner lick your boots _____

Having sex doggy style _____

Please add your own erotic thoughts and fantasies, rate them, and then share them with your partner. You can then switch and let your partner rate and share his fantasies with you.

Sharing your fantasies with your partner is a healthy step in creating a long-lasting and passionate relationship. Already, you are working toward an erotic connection, and all of your energy is focused on each other. Notice how you feel when you share these thoughts with each other.

If it seems too soon to talk about your most private fantasies, just note this information and use it as insight into your own erotic growth. It's important to develop your own erotic and sexual self, and at some point in your relationship, you may feel drawn to share more of yourself with your partner as your own sexual self-esteem and self-confidence increase.

You may notice that some of these issues are things that came up in your monogamy agreement. This is an important point. Learning to expand and work on your sexual monogamy, your fidelity to each other, starts with communication about your fantasies. Growing toward lifelong monogamy is a practice of exploring your erotic life together, and continuing to communicate and expand on your desires. Creating a trusting relationship happens when you each trust that you can share your deepest and most authentic desires. When you can do that, you will feel held and seen in a way that perhaps you never have until now.

CHAPTER 7

Further Explorations in Eroticism

For most couples, intimacy after infidelity seems like an impossible dream or even an improbable nightmare. Intimacy is like a door that swings both ways: it can open to let us in, and it can slam shut to keep us out. Reestablishing intimacy can be a sign that the relationship is working and that trust has been created.

After an affair, you may find that you have shut the door on intimacy to protect yourself. But given that you have come this far in the book, you may now realize that it's possible to move forward and that you may not want to end your current relationship. If you are redefining your monogamy and choosing, for now, to stay together, you will need to create an intimate sex life that not only heals the past but also moves you into an exciting new future—together.

Successful erotic recovery is not determined by how often you have sex, whether or not you have intercourse, how turned on you get, or how many orgasms you may reach. Successful erotic recovery means that you are practicing your eroticism together, that it's a regular and sacred part of your marriage, and that you are more than just roommates. Committing to adventure, sensuality, and intimacy means that your erotic life is always a priority.

Trying Something New

We all need to grow and expand our horizons in many different areas of our lives in order to stay challenged. Sexuality is part of the human experience, and without new ways of developing our erotic selves, we grow tired and frustrated and can even feel stunted in our growth as individuals.

It's important to recognize that for your own sexual growth, trying new things is like maturing in a very important area of your life. If you have a yoga practice or a workout routine, you know that practicing the same things every day can build a strong core and good muscular strength and flexibility. But after a while, your body becomes resistant to change, and you may feel frustrated that you are not stretching into new avenues of health and fitness. Trying new exercises will awaken your body to grow in ways that you recognize almost immediately.

Sexuality is similar concerning the ways that we change. We get stuck in our patterns by sticking to things that work, and we might find that we have been in the maintenance phase of sex for a long time in our relationships. The maintenance phase is where things are maintained at "okay"; you both know how to push all the right buttons, but sex can be boring or predictable. You maintain the consistent routine of having sex, because you know it's good for your relationship and you like to be intimate with one another. But if you stay in the maintenance phase for too long, one or both of you are bound to get frustrated or bored. Sex may have been this way for a while before the affair; it may have been good—but not great. Shaking things up occasionally and trying new things in bed is one way to keep sexuality and intimacy alive.

If You Do What You've Always Done

It's natural to get married to feel safe and secure. We humans naturally seek to form a pair-bond; we seek out partners to create relationships that help us stave off the fears of our daily lives and the difficulties that come from trying to do it all alone. Yet over time, relationships can become so safe and secure that they lose their sense of the unexpected.

When you know that every day, your partner and your routine will be the same as the day before, you can get into what is traditionally known as a "rut." A rut is the exact opposite of what we think of as eroticism. Because eroticism is the opposite of routine, erotic sex includes an edge of danger or the forbidden. By its very nature, erotic sex is naughty and out of the ordinary. Therefore, sex that is split off from erotic fantasy may feel too safe, and can become boring.

Yet we seek safety after an affair, longing to feel comforted in the arms of our partner again. This is fine temporarily, while we establish new boundaries and a new definition of intimacy. But by becoming too attached to that safety, we may actually drive the erotic energy below ground. In the long term, you will want to create a new form of erotic connection that will keep both of you excited, curious, and fulfilled throughout your lives together.

If you do what you've always done, you'll get what you've always gotten. It's time to try something new in your relationship if you want to make it work.

Exploring Your Sexuality

Trying new things sounds easy, but after an affair, it can feel risky and emotionally threatening. What if your partner brings up something she would like to try for the first time, and you think she may have tried this before with the affair partner? Or what if your partner has a fantasy that reminds you that she was cheating with someone who might have already fulfilled that fantasy?

You may need to start slowly with sharing fantasies and moving into a new sensual life together. You may even want to start by remembering that sexuality begins with touching and feeling each other's skin, even each other's breath. Erotic reconnection doesn't have to mean intercourse right away.

Start with Touch

You may need to relearn how to communicate about how to touch each other. Touching and communicating how to touch is a basic skill that can get lost when so much emotional hurt takes place between you. Going back to the basics and learning how your partner likes to be touched and how you like to receive touch is an important (and fun) skill. And what makes this skill even more profound is that you have to learn it without using your words to block the experience.

Keep an Open Mind

Many times we use our intellectual or cognitive processes to dismiss or reject what our partners are doing to us, making it impossible to create a receptive environment for sensual touch. Or we may give feedback to our partners that they interpret as critical, and they may get reactive, which ruins the moment for them too. The following exercise will show you both how to communicate about touch without getting caught in the trap of verbalizing, and it will remind you (and perhaps surprise you) that each of you likes touch in a totally unique and special way.

This exercise doesn't ask you to become too intimate too quickly, so if you are still working on creating a sexual or erotic connection after infidelity has come between you, these are great activities to begin with. Try one or all parts of this exercise this weekend or on your next erotic date night.

Exercise 7.1 Three New Things to Try This Weekend

This exercise consists of three fairly simple activities in erotic and sexual reconnection. Feel free to modify any of these activities to fit your circumstances and emotional states. Just do what feels good! The goal of these activities is to learn to communicate without words. Sometimes our cognitive focus gets in the way of true experience. It may also interfere with our ability to communicate what we like to our partners.

Try these activities together, and choose who will be the sender and who will be the receiver first. Your only job during this exercise is to breathe and to try not to think too hard about how to communicate what you are feeling. You may even have fun; see if you can relax and enjoy the moment.

"Talk Dirty to Me"

Find a comfortable place to sit or lie down across from each other. Take some deep breaths. Be prepared to feel shy or embarrassed, or even to laugh. Have fun with it.

Take turns saying out loud ten dirty words to each other with your eyes open and giving each other full eye contact. Now say ten more.

Many people have never said certain "dirty" words out loud. Give yourself permission to say them. Without using them as punishment or name-calling, you may find that they become sexy and erotic. Or you might find that the dark side of you comes out for a moment, and you enjoy being "dirty" with each other.

This activity has the added benefit of increasing your comfort level with words that you can use during lovemaking in the future.

Naked Trust

If you are making love in your relationship currently, or when you become comfortable with it during your erotic dates, practice alternating being the sender and the receiver during sex. You can do this with massage and sensual touch only, without expectation of sex or intercourse. This is a focused exercise in real trust.

The sender remains fully clothed the whole time while the receiver is completely naked. Practice sensual and sexual generosity as the sender, giving with no expectation of reciprocity. Try massaging your partner or move into more sexual touch. Be conscious that you are giving as an act of generosity so that your partner can experience total pleasure. This can end with orgasm or not.

To improve your ability to be receptive when you make love, practice being the receiver. Practice being open to the receiving, and really try to let in the sensations. Try to be the receiver without guilt or the need to reciprocate in the moment. Let yourself totally relax into the experience and allow the practice of receiving to be just as generous as giving.

Now switch roles and repeat. (You can wait for another night to practice being the sender or switch on the same evening.)

Light Bondage and Control

This activity may be a part of the previous one or done separately. Gently tie up your partner with silk scarves around his wrists. Always tie a wrist or ankle so that the knot doesn't get tighter when pulled. For additional information about safe knot tying, please consult an expert (see the references in my previous book, *Getting the Sex You Want:*

Shed Your Inhibitions and Reach New Heights of Passion Together [Quiver, 2008] for safe ways to play at light bondage, or visit my website, drtammynelson.com). This is important because your partner may struggle playfully during this exercise and pull against the restraints. The scarf could pull and bind, so be careful.

Another version of this exercise is to combine the first and second activities previously presented. Blindfold your partner with a silk scarf and whisper dirty words into his ear. Now take off your partner's clothes, but keep yours on. Massage or touch your partner while you remain clothed and in control. Use feathers, ice cubes, or other objects to give your partner various sensations. With the visual sense blocked by the blindfold, your partner's sense of smell and the feeling on his skin will become heightened and more intense.

Remember to create a safe word when doing any light bondage play. A safe word is a word that you both agree to before the exercise (like "Red"), and not a word that might ordinarily come up in your sex play (such as "Help" or "Stop"). When the partner who is tied up says this word, then the other partner knows it's time to end the game and really stop the activity. This is important, especially when you are just beginning to explore erotic play again after infidelity. Sometimes emotions surface and can become overwhelming. You or your partner may need closeness and comfort during the activity, and you will need to trust that your partner will honor the safe word.

Power

Some couples find that these role-plays and games using power scenarios balance out some of the tension in the relationship after an affair. Be careful that you don't take it to an extreme, using your anger aggressively in the bedroom. But do feel free to playfully enact a little revenge by teasing your partner with a feather or lightly spanking her with your hand as a teasing and playful way to enact a lighthearted "revenge" fantasy. Many couples have reported that they feel a great release of stress when they play out these scenes in loving and safe ways.

When to Challenge Your Sex Life

You may find that you or your partner have many excuses for not working on your sex life together. It may be that one of you is reaching middle age or later life, and you feel that your sex life should be coming to an end anyway.

> Julie and Frank were in their late fifties when Frank admitted he was having an affair with a woman in his office. He was ready to end the affair, and Julie was welcoming him back to the marriage. However, she was not looking forward to dealing with the challenge of working on their sex life together. She admitted that she had never really enjoyed sex with Frank: "Frank and I really never had much of an erotic life together. And I don't see much use in working on one now. I mean, I just turned fifty-six. I guess it's over for me anyway."
>
> For many women, sex gets better than ever in their fifties and sixties. I helped Julie challenge her notion that sex should be over in midlife. I asked if she was in or nearing menopause. "I am in menopause," she responded, "so I don't have to worry about getting pregnant, and I guess that really takes some pressure off. Now I don't have to worry about the messiness or inconvenience. I guess that's a plus.
>
> "Really, I guess I just got bored with our sex life. We always did it the same way, on the same night, and after

about twenty years of Friday night sex in the missionary position, I just thought, *Hey, I'd rather watch TV.*"

Frank wasn't sure he wanted to stay with Julie if she wasn't willing to work on their sex life together. "Picasso fathered a child at ninety," he said. "Not that I want kids, but I'm certainly capable of sex for another forty years. I have just realized that I'm into all kinds of things, and just because I'm a little gray on top doesn't mean a thing. I can actually last longer and enjoy it more than ever before. I just always thought that Julie wasn't a very sexual person, so I went somewhere else. Now I realize it was my fault—well, the fault of both of us, because we never talked about it and never challenged our own ideas about what sex was supposed to be. Now I'm so happy that she wants to stay with me and that we have a chance to begin a new cycle, a new marriage. I love my wife and want to make her happy."

Frank and Julie can challenge their ideas and break out of their negative cycle if they recognize that sometimes, withdrawing from sex can be easier than confronting the need for change. The old way of avoiding their problems may have contributed to Frank's affair. Today they can work on their erotic life together, creating a new and satisfying experience for both of them.

Pushing Your Edge

For many couples, working on a sex life together means pushing past the edge of comfort into new places. This may mean a lot of awkward conversations and new behaviors. It can be difficult to recognize your own sexual needs and even harder to voice them.

For women, repressing or avoiding sexuality may be a result of religious or cultural beliefs. Being nonsexual may make you feel that you are a "good" girl, while acting as a sexual being can make you feel that you are a bad girl. There are many derogatory terms in our culture for women who fully experience their sexuality, "slut" and "whore" being ones that come to mind for many people. The idealistic vision of a woman as a good girl, a mother, a pure Madonna archetype, is the opposite of the "whore" archetype. Some women have a hard time integrating both parts of themselves into their sexuality. They may repress their sexuality in order to be "good" and fit into a society that demands that as wives and mothers, they also be nonsexual beings.

For men, splitting off their sexuality outside of the marriage is one way of protecting their wives from what they may perceive as their own overwhelming or even dangerous levels of erotic energy. If they cannot eroticize their wives, they may feel compelled to put their erotic energy into the "whore" in pornography or into a mistress in an affair. This may, in fact, protect a man's view of his wife as sacred and as the mother of his children. This can be a way of avoiding the mixed feelings that both men and women have of integrating the two roles of family and sexuality.

In marriages in which the partners become parental toward one another, the erotic energy can also become confused. If one partner is bossy or controlling to the other, the relationship can feel as if one partner were the parent and the other the child. Parental relationships quickly become desexualized, and the erotic energy can either go underground or sometimes be diverted outside of the relationship, into an affair.

Pushing the edge of your sexuality means exploring beyond your current comfort level. Do you have difficulty balancing your roles as a parent and a sexual person? Is it hard for you to be a "good" person and a "sexual" person too? How does your partner feel about sex with you? Does he need you to be a good girl or a bad girl in order to get turned on? These are edgy questions.

Can you challenge yourself and ask your partner if he some-times feels bossed around or as if you treat him like a child? Or you may want to confront your partner and share your feelings of being talked down to. This is one way of making sure that the relation-ship remains on an even level, where you both stay in your adult selves. This can be a difficult conversation if the relationship has been in this dynamic for a long while.

Remember, what we avoid talking about will rule us. What we don't deal with will run our lives and make our choices for us. If we don't talk about our fears, we deny the truth in our relationships, and by avoiding the conflict, we let the real issues go underground. Talk to your partner today; push your edge. Use the following dia-logue to help you.

Exercise 7.2   Expand Your Comfort Zone

Answer the following questions in your journal. Find time to share your answers with your partner. Ask your partner to discuss her reactions to your answers. Then have her share her own answers to these ques-tions. Can she answer them honestly as well?

You may need a therapist to help you process some of these issues, especially if some difficult feelings come up for you as a result of this discussion.

What is one fear I have about the role I play in our marriage?

What is one thing I would like to change about myself in our relationship?

What am I most afraid of in my own sexuality?

What is one thing I am afraid my partner will bring up in me sexually?

What is one thing I am afraid that I am unequipped to deal with because of my own unprocessed sexual issues?

Avoiding Boredom

You may be too tired to change things or too shy to ask for what you want. You might get stuck in your own ennui for a while. After an affair, you may find yourself frozen in your own indecision about which way to go in your marriage. One way to break out of this stuck place is to work to make your sex life more exciting. If you hope the sex will get better on its own and assume the intimacy will happen by itself, you are at a critical place. Now is the time to talk about your longings and desires. If you do not, your relationship may cool down. You might even begin to feel bored and blame your partner.

You are responsible for bringing excitement to your marriage. Don't wait for your partner to excite you. You are responsible for making your marriage exciting. If you don't feel excited about your sex life, it may mean that you need not to switch partners but to switch your thoughts about what it takes to make a marriage exciting. We have a tendency to point a finger at our spouses when we are bored and say "I must be bored because you are boring." More likely, we are not getting what we want because we are doing something to prevent it. Are we putting in enough effort to get our needs met? And is it excitement that we crave?

Excitement can mean different things to different people. It may mean that you want adventure or change. Or it might mean that you want risk or danger. Narrow down your definition of excitement so that you can clearly express your desires to your partner. Your partner may think he is giving you exactly what you crave, and yet you may have a totally different idea of what excitement looks like in your sex life.

Don't expect your partner to read your mind. Share clearly and distinctly what excitement means to you. Couples often don't talk about their sex lives, because they assume that their partners should automatically know what they want.

Elaine told her husband, Joe, "If you really loved me, you would know what I want. If I have to tell you what I like, it feels as if you obviously don't even know me *or* don't care." Joe was perplexed: "If you don't tell me, how will we ever learn to please each other?"

Joe is right. Teaching each other what feels good can create a lifetime of erotic connection. This next exercise may help you talk to each other about what you find exciting.

Exercise 7.3   Uncover Your Hidden Fantasies

This exercise will help you flex your fantasy muscles. You are now practicing and becoming more comfortable talking to your partner about sex. Now you have a dialogue structure within which to ask for specific things that you like.

At this point, it's time to get in touch with your own fantasy life. Figuring out your desires and creating a language with which to describe your own fantasies is an important part of educating your partner around what you need.

For this exercise, you are exploring your own fantasy world first, and then sharing these thoughts with your partner. You will need a quiet place to sit down and write, along with paper and a pen, or a journal. Answer the following questions, including as much detail as you can: where you would be, what you would be wearing, what your partner would be doing, and so on.

1.   What is one sexual thing that you love to do?

2.   What is one sexual thing that your partner might want to do?

3.   What is one sexual fantasy that you have that you haven't told your partner about?

Have a dialogue with your partner. Ask for the time to share what you have written. Find a comfortable place to sit or lie down, where you can make eye contact as you share.

Using the Imago dialogue skills from chapter 2, discuss what you have written. Your partner will be the receiver and will listen actively by mirroring, validating, and empathizing. As in the previous exercises, you will be sharing and then mirroring, and then you'll switch roles.

When you have shared and been mirrored, give your partner a chance to validate and empathize. Remember, it might feel as if you each were pushing your comfort level, but mirror and validate your partner's desires. You are an empathetic partner now, and you can listen in this active way to let your partner know that you are receiving what she is saying. You never have to commit to living out your partner's fantasies until you feel comfortable. For now, practice listening, summarizing, validating, and empathizing.

The following is a sample dialogue:

Sender.   One sexual thing that I love to do in bed is _____ .

Receiver,   *simply mirroring and maintaining eye contact.*
          So, one thing that you love to do in bed is _____ .

There are only two responses a receiver needs to make at this point: either "Please send that again," and the sender can repeat what she said so that the receiver can try mirroring again, or mirror what the sender says and then ask simply, "Is there more?"

The sender can say yes and send more or "No, you got it" and stop there. After the receiver has mirrored, the sender switches and becomes the receiver.

Now it's time to summarize and validate, and using the sentence stem "It makes sense to me _____" makes this easier. How does it make sense to you, knowing your partner as you do, that your partner would like these things and want to do more of them with you?

Receiver. So what I heard you say was _____
[summarize].

Now validate.

Receiver. It makes sense to me that you would want _____
[validation]. Knowing you the way I do, I can understand
why you would desire that _____ .

Now comes the empathy, which is simply an educated guess at
how you think your partner would feel about these desires and
fantasies.

Receiver. And I can imagine that if we did those things, it would
make you feel _____ [add feelings]. Is there
more?

Now switch roles so that both of you will have had a turn at summarizing, validating, and empathizing.

You can move on from here if you are both comfortable and each of you can choose one thing that you are open to trying that your partner has expressed a desire for.

Remember that you are giving your partner the gift of hearing her fantasy. You may even want to live out your partner's fantasy by acting on it, but before you can do this, you have to hear your partner's thoughts, feelings, and desires. If now is not a good time or you find that you need further dialogue to empathize, ask for another time to discuss your desires and fantasies further. Making a plan to keep talking until your partner understands you can allow for openness and trust in the relationship. There's no rush. Just hearing about your sexual and erotic desires might add enough spark and excitement that making love spontaneously becomes a definite possibility.

Boredom is an excuse for not trying. If you find that you are feeling bored with your erotic life or your new monogamy relationship, it may be that you have hit a wall in your own development. Exploring your own sexuality can sometimes bring up things that are difficult to look at and that you may not even know you have had trouble with.

Sometimes an affair may have been a way of avoiding doing that work all along. Now is the time for *you* to do the work, regardless of whether you, your partner, or both of you cheated. Gaining insight into your own issues will help you explore your own sexuality and bring it into your partnership in a healthy and exciting new way. The following exercise may help.

Exercise 7.4 Sexual Insight

This exercise will help you explore and identify your own sexual needs, thoughts, and fantasies, and learn to talk about them.

Using the Imago dialogue technique, sit down with your partner when you have some time to talk without distractions. You will use the same technique of taking turns as the sender and the receiver. One of you, the sender, will send your thoughts using this dialogue as an outline to help you. The receiver will mirror, and then validate and emphasize. Then you will switch so that the receiver becomes the sender, and repeat.

The dialogue may go something like this:

Insight

Sender. I am trying to understand my sexual needs and explore my sexuality.

Receiver. *mirroring.* So you are trying to understand your sexual needs and explore your sexuality. Is there more?

Sender. One fantasy I have that I would like to take into action or explore is _____ .

Receiver. *mirroring.* One fantasy you have that you would like to act out or explore is _____ .

Sender. I think if we did act out this fantasy, it would fill my need for _____ .

Receiver. *mirroring.* You think if we did act out this fantasy, it would fill your need for _____ .

Validation

Receiver. It makes sense that you have this fantasy, because _____ . And it makes sense that if we did this, it would fill your need, because _____ . It also makes sense that your fantasies might be different from mine.

Empathy

Receiver. I imagine that if we did act out this fantasy or need, you would feel _____ .

Generosity

Sender. I am open to being present and communicating my needs.

Receiver. You are open to being present and communicating your needs. [If comfortable] I am open to your sexual fantasies. You deserve to have them.

Sender. Thank you for being open.

Long-term partnerships don't have to be boring. You may think you know everything about your partner, especially if you have been together for a long time. Yet sexually we grow all the time, in many new and intriguing ways. You can help your partner find out how he can grow and you can explore your own growth by capitalizing on what is familiar between you and, at the same time, avoiding taking each other for granted.

Many people say they had a feeling of "being taken for granted" or feeling "unappreciated" right before they cheated. Some said they had stopped appreciating what they had. Feeling taken for granted means that they felt that their partners had stopped being curious about them. They had stopped wondering and expecting anything new or interesting, and expected things to be the same all the time. When someone new comes along asking about who you are and what you like, and wanting to know all about you, that curiosity can be intriguing and hard to resist.

The work you are doing together in this book is a way of creating a new curiosity between you. Asking questions, sharing fantasies, and exploring new adventures will trigger new possibilities that you may never have known existed in your old relationship.

Adventure as an Infidelity Intervention

One of the most important *infidelity interventions* that you can continue into the future of your relationship is creating "relationship adventure." Creating new and exciting experiences that shake up your routine is important. It's not just something you read about in a pithy article in a magazine while waiting in the grocery line. You have to actually do it. Adding adventure to your sex life is crucial.

But shaking the very roots of your love life can be scary. And yet rocking your love life can be healthy. Adding erotic experiences that challenge you and provide new adventures is important to creating a new and lasting monogamy together. As you form a vision of your future, add this new assignment: try to create a new sexy adventure once a month. Adventure means that you might try something edgy or even a little scary. If you are used to having sex only in the bedroom, try the kitchen counter or even the backyard one night in the dark. Take your erotic date night to the backseat of the car as you did when you were young, or try a camping trip to the mountains and rough it in the woods. Add some new sex toys or a leather outfit. Have sex suspended from a sex swing bolted to the ceiling. Whatever your idea of adventure might be, try doing something totally new once a month. It not only adds adrenaline to your lovemaking, but also sends your dopamine and serotonin levels up, as well as your sex hormones (like testosterone), which add to the excitement of your lovemaking and create some of the thrill that you may crave in your new monogamous relationship.

If you have a more open agreement in your marriage, try sharing your erotic adventure with another couple or watching other people at a sex club. Talk about how you want to share your new experiences, and make a plan today for your next date night.

Filling Your Home with Erotic Energy

Remember that your partner, like you, is a deep and complex person with many layers to explore and cultivate. What you don't know about your partner may surprise you. You may only now be discovering that your partner is not the person you imagined she was. And it's time to find out some of the new areas your partner has been cultivating in herself.

Encouraging your partner to bring her erotic energy home means nurturing an environment that welcomes adventure and exploration.

Flirting as an Appetizer

Starting over can be difficult. Beginning a new erotic relationship between you can feel like starting from scratch. As in any new relationship, seduction many times begins with flirting. One way to encourage your partner to bring her sexiness home is by revisiting some of that flirtatious energy. Do you remember how to flirt with each other? Flirting is a way of teasing, reminding each other about the erotic pleasure that awaits at home. Remind your partner that she has more to look forward to than just kids and chores. Entice her with seduction. Pleasure is always seductive, so let your partner know the ways you are going to make her feel good: whisper in her ear, text her, leave her notes. Make your partner your mistress, and let her know that there's no one else you'd rather be with, tonight or any other night.

Compromise

"Compromise" is a word that couples throw around when they decide they want to work things out after an affair. They decide that if neither of them can get their way, then they will "compromise," and at least one of them will get a little of what he or she wants. But instead of both partners being at least a little happy, often both end up feeling disappointed. *Compromising* means that you both are giving up what you want, but you are trying to be fair about it. *Negotiating* means that you are talking about your needs and trying to come up with a fair enough bargain.

But many couples negotiate and bargain with sex. These negotiations can be spoken or unspoken: "If you clean the garage, I'll have sex." "If you do the dishes, I will have more sex with you." "If you give up the outside boyfriend, I will work harder to make you happy in bed." "If you will give me more oral sex, I will take you out to dinner more often." "I will refuse to have sex with you until you at least put some effort into our relationship."

All of these power struggles only use sex as a way to keep score, and keeping score drives couples apart. What you long for from each other is real and valid, and has deep meaning for you as individuals. It is in the striving to provide these needs for one another that the relationship will grow in the long run. Stop keeping score. Don't use sex as a bargaining tool. Talk directly about your needs and wants. Keep your conversation about your desires open and ongoing. In the long run, both of you have more of a chance of getting your needs met when you are transparent about your feelings and fantasies. And neither of you will have to compromise on what you long for, if you can find empathy for one another.

Adventure, Sensuality, and Intimacy

The three keys to a long and healthy erotic life together are adventure, sensuality, and intimacy. Adventure, as we have discussed, is a vital part of a mature love life. Add in adventure regularly, and you will look forward to making love with your partner, adding creativity to a satisfying romantic life. Sensuality means that romance and eroticism become one and the same, that your physical experience with one another is pleasing to all of your senses, and that pleasure is a regular part of your shared life together. And intimacy means that you will find a new emotional depth, a passion for one another, and you will feel seen by your partner, in deep and meaningful ways. When you have these three elements in your erotic life and make them your goals, you will be on a path toward a more satisfying future.

CHAPTER 8

Your New Relationship, Moving Forward

It can take several years and sometimes longer to get past an affair, and some couples never get over the hurt or damage it does to their relationships. And yet the honesty that you are working on with the help of the exercises in this book can make you feel closer to each other than ever. This will help determine the outcome of your relationship more than any statistics about who cheats, how they got caught, or how long the affairs lasted. Repairing and starting again in a new relationship with your current partner can reveal a new, more mature side of each of you. More aware and insightful individuals make for a more intimate and connected couple.

If you remain accessible to your partner and open to discussions about your vision for the future, and if you both have the willingness to constantly change and adjust according to your relationship needs, you have the foundation of a shared future life together. If you commit to a shared erotic life going forward, regardless of your age or physical sexual functioning, the number of positive, pleasurable, and fulfilling years you can share together is determined only by how long you live.

It's hard to predict whether you are one of the lucky couples who will make it through this process. Some days you may wonder about the outcome of all of this hard work. And other days you may find yourself looking back and feeling that you two are closer than ever and have a solid new relationship. Only you and your partner can decide whether you will make it. This decision is one that you must make together every day.

There are some indicators, however, of whether you will be able to make it work as a couple going forward. Following the infidelity interventions in this book will help improve your chances for survival as a couple.

1. Have you each taken some responsibility for how your relationship got to this point? Have you had insight into your own behaviors and what led to the affair?

2. Have you shared your vision of a new future together and taken the time to sit down and create a new monogamy agreement? Have you talked about the fluidity of your monogamy continuum, clearly delineating what is meaningful for each of you in your new life together?

3. Are you working on your erotic recovery, by having an erotic date night once a week and talking about fantasies, creating adventure, and moving toward sensuality and intimacy?

If you answered yes to all three indicators, chances are you are already making it. And you are well on your way to redefining your relationship after the infidelity and on your way to experiencing long-term recovery from your affair.

How to Cope with the New Agreement

If you can't cope with your new agreement for any reason—morally, ethically, or emotionally, or it doesn't feel right for any reason—put your agreement on hold.

Talk with your partner and decide whether the agreement is too strict for you, because it doesn't align with your values or because it somehow doesn't reflect your own integrity. Or, maybe you are really done with your relationship after all, and this was purely an experiment to see if you could keep it going. It's time to be honest with yourself and trust your own intuition. You have grown enough by now to know whether your fear is driving your decisions or your inner voice is telling you the truth. If you aren't sure, go back to the exercises in chapter 3, where you learned to sit quietly and listen to your inner voice. Try to find that place inside that tells you what you need to know, and decide for yourself where your intuition is leading you.

Living One Day at a Time

You may not know whether you are making the right decision. But know that you have decided, for now, that you will be in a monogamous relationship with your spouse—just for today. And whatever that means for you, stick with your decision for this twenty-four-hour period before changing your mind. One way to look at it is that once you decide for today that you will be in your new monogamy relationship with your partner, try not to question your own judgment. You are already in the boat for today. The boat has left the shore. You are sailing down the river, and until you have stepped off the boat and onto the deck at the end of this day, you are committed to your decision to be with this person.

Monogamy is a decision you make every day. You don't make it once in your lifetime and live happily ever after. You make your monogamy commitment every morning when you wake up, and trust your decision that this is what's right for you this day, with this person.

If you aren't sure, just for today, try to just be on the boat. Worry about what will happen tomorrow when tomorrow gets here. You can always get off the boat then. But there's no point in worrying about what will happen when you get to shore when you're not even there yet. Enjoy the ride, feel the flow of the river, and be in your relationship fully—just for today.

What to Do If It's Not Working

If you decide at any point that your new monogamy isn't working, either because your agreement isn't what you thought it would be or because your clauses are too restrictive or too loose, make a time to sit down with your partner to discuss your feelings. Don't avoid the conflict out of fear. And don't stay in the boat because you're afraid to get out. Stay in it because you have decided that for today this is where you want to be. But if, at any time, you feel the need for a discussion, initiate one.

Finding Each Other Again

It's important to talk to your partner about your feelings. Find one another when you need to connect. Create this new relationship on a foundation of shared emotions and experiences.

What do you want to create now in your new relationship? Going back to the relationship you used to have will only get you what you had in the past. Plan for your new marriage and decide together what that will look like. Talk about your new sex life, your new emotional life, and your new recreational life. How will you connect now that will be different from last time? Have some fun discussing your longings and your desires. Get in touch with your own needs and try to validate your partner's needs. Make the envisioning of your future an ongoing plan that you revisit often, even every day if you can.

These factors—talking, feeling, and envisioning—will move you forward and help you take advantage of the shake-up in your relationship. If you need extra help to do these steps, contact a qualified professional in your area to help you move things along.

To find a therapist who is open and supportive, and can help you with your new monogamy agreement, look for someone who is empathetic to flexible definitions of monogamy. Find a therapist who doesn't polarize relationships after an affair to consist of one "good guy" and one "bad guy." Watch out for experts who tell you they have the answer to "why all men cheat" or "why women have affairs," because there is no one reason why anyone cheats. People have affairs for many different reasons, and what's most important is figuring out what you will do about it now that you are working on your new monogamy.

For help finding a therapist to work with if you are in an open marriage, contact your local polyamory group. If an open relationship is not included in your vision but you want to find a counselor who will really move your relationship forward, look for a therapist who is certified in Imago Relationship Therapy because this type of professional can help you use the tools outlined in this book.

It's realistic to expect monogamy in whatever way you desire it in your relationship now and in the future. Will you get it? That's a different question altogether. The answer is determined by your ability to communicate with each other and manage your expectations going forward. Monogamy is a practice. Like yoga, it takes years to get it right. And you may never stand on your head. But every day, if you breathe, stretch, and move a little past your comfort zone, you can grow into something new. Practice your monogamy and make it something you commit to every day.

The Future of Monogamy

We are culturally and socially driven to expect monogamy in marriage. We have explicit as well as implicit expectations and assume that our partners agree with us when we take our vows, even if we never discuss the exact meanings of the vows first.

Yet monogamy is changing in this century. Our built-in expectations are fast becoming outdated and no longer apply. Marriage as we know it is changing. It's the newest frontier in the rapidly expanding growth of our new century. What makes us think that everything else will change in this century but marriage should stay the same as it was for our grandparents? It won't. And the couples that manage to stay together and make it work will be the ones who decide to create fluidity and flexibility in their partnerships, and find ways to make monogamy work for them.

I call this new age of relationships the "new monogamy," because our definition of commitment has yet to catch up to what's actually happening in our culture. Our ability to remain monogamous is becoming more difficult in an age when cheating is easier than ever. We have access to infidelity possibilities constantly: on our laptops, smartphones, and other handheld devices.

With half of us still divorcing and marrying again, it's obvious that we want to be in committed partnerships; that hasn't changed. But we are waiting; we are marrying later than ever. And people who marry sometimes cheat and lie about keeping that commitment. Yet we remain hopeful. Our idealism is reflected in the fact that we are still trying. We want to desire the same person for a lifetime, but we don't know how to make that work. We have lots of ideas and education in our society on how to cheat but, until now, not much information on how to stay monogamous.

This book is a response to a growing need. Many couples are developing a new monogamy in the face of the difficulties of staying true to each other in committed relationships. In my office and in my workshops and retreats, I see hundreds of couples from varied backgrounds who are negotiating their monogamy after infidelity and making it work. These fluid definitions of monogamy are defined by new types of communication that make it easier to talk about the rules. This is a new revolution in marriage, never seen before.

The new monogamy means that after an affair, you can stay together. Sometimes the grass is not greener on the other side. Divorce is not always the best option. Rewriting your monogamy agreement by sitting down and openly discussing expectations going forward can save your marriage and even propel it forward.

The future is bright. The places where pain and hurt have scarred you are where you can hold the most love. No matter how you have been wounded, know that you are moving through it and moving toward love.

Don't forget to breathe.

References

Atwood, Joan D., and Limor Schwartz. 2002. "Cyber-Sex: The New Affair Treatment Considerations." *Journal of Couple and Relationship Therapy* 1 (3):37–56.

Bennett, Jessica. 2009. "Only You. And You. And You. Polyamory—Relationships with Multiple, Mutually Consenting Partners—Has a Coming-Out Party." *Newsweek* Web Exclusive, July 29. www.newsweek.com/id/209164/page/1.

Ben-Zeev, Aaron. 2008. "Proclaimed Monogamy with Clandestine Adultery." *Psychology Today*, Nov 21. www.psychologytoday.com/node/2450.

Charny, Israel, and Sivan Parnass. 1995. "The Impact of Extramarital Relationships on the Continuation of Marriages." *Journal of Sex and Marital Therapy* 21 (2):100–115.

Cooper, Robert K. 2000. "A New Neuroscience of Leadership: Bringing Out More of the Best in People." *Strategy and Leadership Journal* 28 (6):11–15.

Halper, Jan. 1988. *Quiet Desperation: The Truth about Successful Men*. New York: Warner Books.

Hendrix, Harville. 2008. *Getting the Love You Want: A Guide for Couples*. New York: Henry Holt and Company.

Masters, William H., Virginia E. Johnson, and Robert C. Kolodny. 1986. *On Sex and Human Loving*. Boston: Little, Brown and Company.

Nelson, Tammy. 2010. "The New Monogamy: How Far Should We Go?" *Psychotherapy Networker*, July/August. http://www.psycho therapynetworker.org/component/content/article/222-2010 -julyaugust/926-the-new-monogamy

Spring, Janis A. 1996. *After the Affair: Healing the Pain and Rebuilding Trust When a Partner Has Been Unfaithful*. With Michael Spring. New York: HarperCollins Publishers.

Tammy Nelson, PhD, is a world-renowned expert in relationships, a psychotherapist in private practice, and a popular lecturer around the world on sexuality and human relationships and global relational change. She is a board-certified sexologist, an AASECT-certified sex therapist, a licensed professional counselor, and a certified Imago relationship therapist. She resides in the New York City area, where she works in her private practice treating couples who are looking to restore passion to their relationships, recover from infidelity, and create their new monogamy, one agreement at a time.

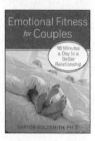

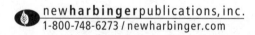